CULTURAL MARKETS AND UTILITY PROVIDERS

CULTURAL MARKETS AND UTILITY PROVIDERS

A Study of a Religious Site in India

Atanu Sengupta
Krishanu Nath

KALPAZ

ISBN: 978-93-5128-056-9

Price: ₹ 630

First Published, 2015

Published by

Kalpaz Publications
C-30, Satyawati Nagar,
Delhi - 110052
E-mail: kalpaz@hotmail.com
Ph.: 9212142040

Laser Typesetting : Rajender Vashist, Delhi
Printed at : G. Print Process, Delhi

Cataloging in Publication Data—DK
Courtesy: D.K. Agencies (P) Ltd. <docinfo@dkagencies.com>

Sengupta, Atanu, 1967- **author.**
Cultural markets and utility providers : a study of a religious site in India / Atanu Sengupta, Krishanu Nath.
pages cm
Includes bibliographical references (pages) and index.
ISBN 9789351280569

1. Hindu temples—Economic aspects—India—Tarakeswar. 2. Hindu pilgrims and pilgrimages—Economic aspects—India—Tarakeswar. 3. Tarakeswar (India)—Religion—Economic aspects. 4. Cultural industries—India—Tarakeswar. I. Nath, Krishnu, author. II. Title.

DDC 294.535095414 23

Contents

Foreword 7
Preface 9
Acknowledgements 11
Introduction 13

1. Religion, Culture and Economics 15
2. The Economics of Temple Culture: A Short Introduction 55
3. Some Earlier Studies 59
4. Data Used in the Study 71
5. Workers, Consumers and Providers in the 'Sacred' Market 73
6. Estimating the Demand for a Cultural Good: A Study of a Religious Site Using Count Data 133
7. Unskilled Workers in the Cultural Market: A Case Study of the Utility Providers at a Religious Site 155
8. Main Findings and Conclusion 177

Bibliography 181
Photo Gallery 189
Index 195

Foreword

The entire research study on cultural economics especially emphasises on Temple Culture, with reference to a case study of Tarakeswar. It is terminated by giving the conclusion that the socio-economic development of Tarakeswar block as well as municipality is fully dependent upon the Religious Culture of the temple of '*Baba Taraknath*'. The municipal authority, the railway authority and various local hospitality groups at Tarakeswar are socio-economically dependent on the Temple Culture to a great extent. We have summarised the main results in each chapter on the relevant aspects of Temple Culture.

Preface

In the modern parlance, livelihood has been defined in a number of ways. However, essentially it measures the income flow and the resilience of the income earner under adversity. In the modern world, livelihood is generated of a wide spectrum of sources—some outside the well-defined arena of main stream economics. Often cultural activities generate livelihood opportunity for a number of semi-skilled and un-skilled workers related to it. Here the culture plays a pivotal role creating an income earning space for those who would have otherwise find it difficult to ensure it.

In many sacred centres, people acquire religion in the same way as they acquire other objects of their choice and they also evaluate its costs and benefits and acts so as to optimise its utility. It determines the content of religious commodities and the structure, where religion is unregulated and as a result, a competition among religious firms is pronounced. Here along with considerable portions of the people inside or outside of this centre earn their livelihood by providing different types of secular and non-secular services to them.

In our study, we have selected Tarakeswar—a Hindu pilgrimage site in West Bengal, India—for analysing the socio-economic pattern and nature of local hospitality provider is allied with the religious culture. Economic pattern of this sacred centre depends upon the occupational structure, standard of living of the inhabitants of the town, social economic infrastructural conditions, etc. The occupational profile reflects that at Tarakeswer, too, a substantial portion of population earns their livelihood from the temple as well as from the pilgrims and also the nature and extent of dependency vary from one group to the other.

This study, we hope, will be useful to researchers, policy-makers, academicians as well as general public who are interested in the interaction between culture and economy.

Atanu Sengupta
Krishanu Nath

Acknowledgements

The authors wish to acknowledge the help provided by the University authority particularly the Honourable Vice Chancellor Prof Smritikumar Sarkar in giving us the ample opportunity to carry on the research activity. We would also like to thank the Faculties of the Economics Department, particularly Professor Arup Kumar Chattopadhyay, Professor Maniklal Adhikari and Profesosor Souymendra Kishore Dutta for various helpful suggestions in preparing this study. We also thank the employees of the Tarakeswar temple, pilgrims and others for patiently answering our queries. Any suggestions are welcome.

Introduction

The word 'culture' is a derivative of '*cult*' by adding the suffix '*ure*'. However, that cult is derived from the Latin '*cultus*' through the French 'culte', means on organised system of religious worship or ceremonial, and the allied word 'culture' can't be its derivative. But the current meaning of 'culture', given by the New English Oxford dictionary, is the rearing or rising of certain animals or of natural products. The word 'culture' means the cultivating or development (of the mind, faculties, manners)—improvement or refinement by education and training.

In the traditional economics, production activity is independent on the consumption activity and they occur at different points of time. In the definition of Care Economics, presented by Arrow, the act of consumption is related with the act of production. There are two parts of Care Economics. These are Secular Part and Cultural Part. For example, medical care falls under the secular part of Care Economics. Suppose a patient visits a doctor for cure of a particular disease. The act of consumption that leads to the recovery is related with the process of doctor's continuous advice and prescriptions, which constitute the production of the service, the patient does not know much about the quality of service. Again there is a basic asymmetry. The doctor knows more about the diseases and its probable cure than the patient. For making this market efficient, some ethical standards are necessary. Without faith in doctor, the patient can't be fully satisfied. In his cure may be affected by his faith in the doctor's popularity, no placable effect.

Under Cultural Economics, there is an extra dimension. Added with the moral restrictions, there is a need for active participation of the consumer in the generation process. Suppose a classical dancer performs. The demand for such a performance will depend not only on the positive and negative externality, but also on the spectator's readiness to enjoy the performance itself. In the cultural term, Aristotle called this 'sympathy' – a process, in which the viewer sympathises with the situation, created by the performer. In a sense, a spectator is also a part of the performance.

Under secular part of Care Economics, consumers are passive but producers are active. So, we can measure benefits, which arise from the demand-supply interaction. On the other hand, under cultural part, both the consumers and producers are active. That is, both the activities are generated simultaneously from the market by the active participation, the greater is his/her benefit.

Textbook economics teaches us that the demand for any commodity is related to the utility that it gives. Cultural goods provide utility that is specific to certain cultural milieu. Goods and services that may appear strange to "outsiders" have a meaningful existence in the eye of the beholder. However, once the cultural sphere is defined, the standard law of demand and supply operates. This is what observed by Adam Smith in his discussions on religion in the *Wealth of Nations.*

In this book, we are concerned with the demand for a specific cultural good—the demand for pilgrimage activities at Tarakeswar, a religious site of West Bengal. The demand is highly culture specific; it is valuable only to those who are devotionally attached to such practices. However, given this affinity, the demand-supply mechanism operates as in ordinary economics.

1

Religion, Culture and Economics

1.1 Introduction

In the modern parlance, livelihood has been defined in a number of ways. However, essentially it measures the income flow and the resilience of the income earner under adversity. In the modern world, livelihood is generated of a wide spectrum of sources—some outside the well-defined arena of main stream economics. Often cultural activities generate livelihood opportunity for a number of semi-skilled and un-skilled workers related to it. Here the culture plays a pivotal role creating an income earning space for those who would have otherwise find it difficult to ensure it.

In many sacred centres, people acquire religion in the same way that they acquire other objects of their choice and they also evaluate its costs and benefits and acts so as to optimise its utility. It determines the content of religious commodities and the structure, where religion is unregulated and as a result, a competition among religious firms is pronounced. Here along with considerable portions of the people inside or outside of this centre earn their livelihood by providing different types of secular and non-secular services to them.

Through the discussion of economic behaviour, religious culture is classified from two different aspects—demand side and supply side of this particular culture[1]. From demand side, this culture is consumed by the devotees who arrive to this place to fulfill their religious requirements and also their mental and virtuous pleasure. On the contrary, from the supply side, these demands are fulfilled by the various types of beneficiary groups which are classified into two categories—the group of sacred associates like priests, pilgrim guides and the group of secular associates like rest house owners, shopkeepers, restaurant owners, florists, potters, etc.

In our study, we have selected Tarakeswar—a Hindu pilgrimage site in West Bengal, India—for analysing the socio-economic pattern and nature of local hospitality providers allied with the religious culture. Economic pattern of this sacred centre depends upon the occupational structure, standard of living of the inhabitants of the town, social-economic infrastructural conditions, etc. The occupational profile reflects that at Tarakeswer, too, a substantial portion of population earns their livelihood from the temple as well as from the pilgrims and also the nature and extent of dependency vary from one group to the other.

1.2 Some Conceptual Issues

The word 'culture' is a derivative of 'cult' by adding the suffix 'ure'. However, that cult is derived from the Latin *'cultus'* through the French *'culte'*, means 'an organised system of religious worship or ceremonial', and the allied word 'culture' can't be its derivative. But the current meaning of 'culture', given by the New English Oxford dictionary, is 'the rearing or rising of certain animals or of natural products'. The word 'culture' means 'the cultivating or development (of the mind, faculties, manners) – improvement or refinement by education and training'.

In the traditional economics, production activity is independent on the consumption activity and it occurs at different points of time. In the definition of Care Economics, presented by Arrow, the act of consumption is related with the act of production. There are two parts of 'Care Economics'. These are Secular Part and Cultural Part. For example, medical care falls under the secular part of Care Economics. Suppose, a patient visits a doctor for cure of a particular disease. The act of consumption that leads to the recovery is related with the process of doctor's continuous advices and prescriptions, which constitute the production of the service. In fact, there is a basic uncertainty. Before fully consuming the service, the patient does not know much about the quality of service. Again, there is a basic asymmetry. The doctor knows more about the diseases and its probable cure than the patient. For making this market efficient, some ethical standards are necessary. Without faith in doctor, the patient can't be fully satisfied. Even his cure may be affected by his faith in the doctor's popularity, no placable effect. Arrow sights one important word by Sapiro, where he had shown, even in the erstwhile Soviet Union, patients preferred some doctors rather than others though the mechanism was State-funded. This importance of morality, faith and placable in the care industry also have some external effect. Good reputation which results from positive externality may help boost-up a doctor's demand, while negative externality tends to dampen it. Also, there is a multiplier effect, because more is the doctor's demand, more is the need for attendants and other semi-skilled persons. However, there is requirement of some external forces (apart from the market mechanism) to control the quality. Otherwise, the negative externality will operate as demand exceeds below a point so as to exhaust the doctor's capacity. The same logic may be applied to a medical institute also. Other care sectors, such as education, governance, etc., also fall under this category.

Under Cultural Economics, there is an extra dimension. Added with the moral restrictions, there is a need for active participation of the consumer in the generation process. Suppose, a classical dancer performs. The demand for such a performance will depend not only on the positive and negative externality, but also on the spectator's readiness to enjoy the performance itself. In the cultural term, Aristotle called this 'sympathy'. A process, in which the viewer sympathises with the situation, created by the performer. In a sense, a spectator is also a part of the performance.

Under secular part of Care Economics, consumers are passive but producers are active. So, we can measure benefits, which arise from the demand-supply interaction. On the other hand, under cultural part, both the consumers and producers are active. That is, both the activities are generated simultaneously from the market by the active participation of the consumers. Here the benefit is non-measurable. The more consumer's participation, the greater is his/her benefit.

This can be shown by the following diagram (1). In this figure, the two sets are represented by the activity of consumption (C) and activity of production (P). Under Traditional Economics in diagram 1(b) both sets can't intersect each other, since they are independent. But both the sets under Care Economics intersect each other, since the act of consumption is related with act of production and both the activities are generated simultaneously in the market, represented by the intersection of both the sets in Fig.1.

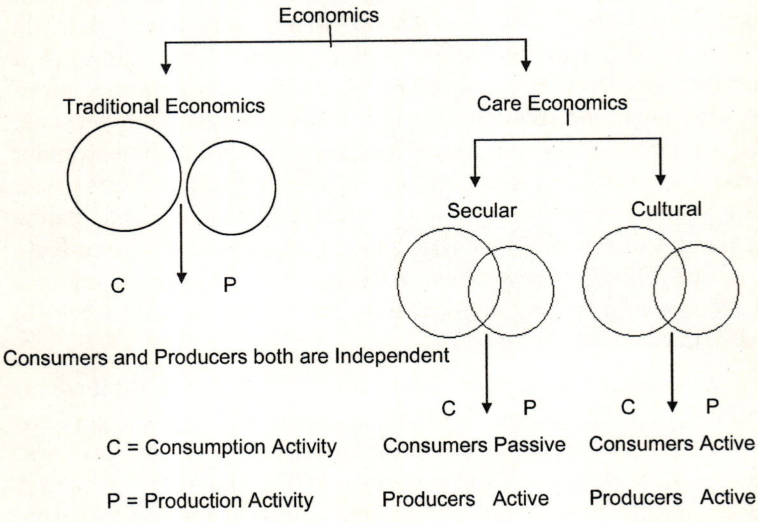

Fig. 1(a) Fig. 1(b)

Fig. 1: Different Concepts of Economics.

By the 'culture', we mean culture of the human races, i.e., Human Culture. The Human Cultural is defined as the human behaviour of individuals. It implies that the human characteristics of a human for being a human. The Human Culture consists of four other cultures. These are Social, Economic and Political Cultures.

Social Culture: It is the social norm that is generated from the society. It includes certain components like demography, education, caste, occupation, family and religion. The demographic characteristics of the Social Culture also include age, sex, marital status, etc.

Religious Culture: It is the foundation, the backbone, the life-centre of the society. With some it is politics, with others it is social culture; others again may have intellectual culture and so on for their national background. But this religious culture alone for its basis, for its backbone, for the bedrock upon which the whole building of its life has been based. Religious and every thing else must become subordinate to that one principal theme of its life. This culture is created from the worship of God of a particular religion.

Economic Culture: All the economic activities are generated from the Economic Culture, which is indispensable for the human life. Economic Culture represents a broad outline of the working life of different occupational groups to show their nature of economic involvement with the society. This culture implies the interaction between demand and supply of various goods and services provided by the income generating units (i.e., people) to maintain their livelihood.

Political Culture: This culture is totally heterogeneous sub-group of Human Culture. Every people associated with the different political activities, directly or indirectly, rather religious activities, which are not a matter of our discussion. Yet we cannot avoid this.

Besides these, there is another culture, named as Temple Culture, under Religious Culture.

Temple Culture: Most interesting feature is that the Temple Culture is the sub-set of Religious Culture. Temple is a sign of deity, which presides the place as pilgrimage. There is a mutual action between various cultural agents, who provide this culture to the society and pilgrims, who consume it. The formation and development of Temple Culture is from a particular temple. Under this culture, it was observed that the population of the area surrounding the temple had certain behavioural pattern and economic activities from the rest of the people of the town. This is mainly because they are mostly associated with the religious activities of the temple in some form or the other. The inter-relationship of sacred centres from locational perspective has also been examined.

1.3 Interaction among Different Cultures

Under Human Culture, there is a relationship among these four cultures. In fig. (1), Human Culture is a universal set, and all the four sets—Religious Culture, Economic Culture, Social Culture and Political Culture—are the sub-sets of this universal set of Human Culture. All these sub-sets intersect each other, except one set, i.e., Political Culture, since Political Culture is only related to the Economic Culture and it has almost no relation with other Cultures. To represent the economics of Temple Culture, we are sliding up the intersection region between Temple Culture and Economic Culture, shown by a shaded region in Fig. 2.

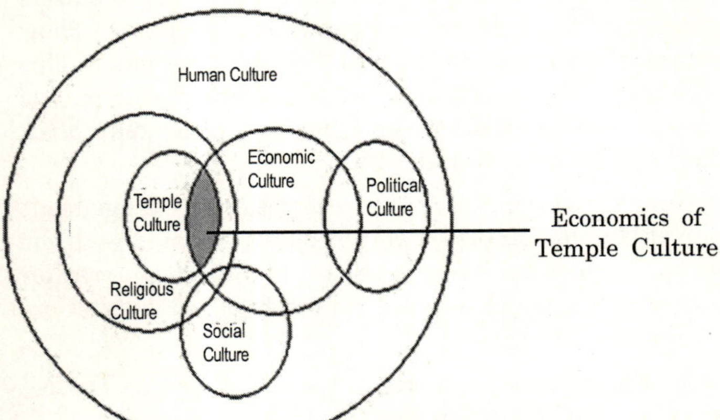

Fig. 2: Interaction among Temple Culture, Social Culture and Economic Culture.

Now, we examine how the Economic Culture is related to the Temple Culture, by the help of schematic Fig. 3.

We have already said that Human Culture is divided into four parts and they are interrelated, except the Political Culture. In the society, both Social Culture and the Economic Culture are defined by the Religious Culture. Under Social Structure, the most important feature is caste-system. The various caste-groups have different degrees of social prestige, which is correlated with a host of other socio-cultural and economic factors. For example, the white-collar occupation such as teachers, clerks, doctors, engineers, inspectors, supervisors, station-masters, priests, etc. are mainly confined to the high-caste household members. Different types of business, skilled activities, i.e., from pretty trade to large trade, are done by the middle-caste groups.

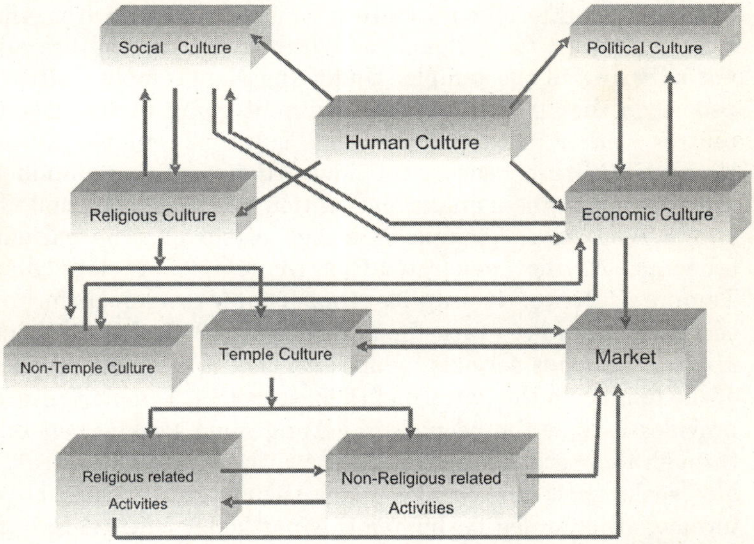

Fig. 3: Inter-relation among Different Parts of Human Culture through Market.

The low caste people do all types of manual and un-skilled works. This finding implies that the low-caste people have relatively poor economic condition and high-caste people have better economic condition. Again, humans under different social structures have presided by their corresponding religious system with heterogeneous faith. Different religious cultures such as Buddhism, Jainism, Hinduism, Mohammedanism, Christians, etc. have different social cultures. Yet there is a social diversity in the status among *Brahmans, Kshatriyas, Vaishyas* and *Shudras* under a particular religious category, Hindu. So, the social culture is dominated by the religious culture. There is another sub-culture, i.e., Political Culture, which is only related to the Economic Culture. We know the politically cultured country is always economically strong, whether it is a totally different aspect from the point of view of our analysis.

In this project, we will focus on the interaction between Hindu Religious Culture and Economic Culture. In Fig. (3), Religious Culture is divided into two parts. These are (a) Non-Temple Culture and (b) Temple Culture. Non-Temple Culture is defined as the religious culture which is defended from the temple. That is, the religious activities under this culture are not adhering to the temple. Under the Non-Temple Culture, people do their ritual activities without going to the sacred centres, rather in their home. This culture is related to the Economic Culture, because religious activities of these families are afforded by their financial condition. On the other hand, in Hindu religion, the temple is a sign of shrine. The various economic activities, generated from the temple, are defined as Temple Culture. It implies that people under different occupational groups earn their livelihood by offering different kinds of religious services, which reveals the economic impact of the temple on the pattern of their activities. Temple Culture provides us how the people are getting some sorts of benefits through their economic involvement with the sacred centre. It also seeks, how the people, under their subsistence level of income, are afforded for buying this particular culture. In Fig. (2), the Temple Culture is also divided into two parts: (a) Religious Activities, and (b) Non-Religious Activities. The religious activities imply the different types of ritual activities associated with a particular religion. For instance, in case of Hindu religion, it includes the activities of the group of sacred specialists like monastic, pundits, priests and pilgrims, and also the activities of other ritual associates such as pilgrim guides, barbers, potters, florists, rest-house owners, shopkeepers, restaurant owners, hawkers, fruit-sellers and different menial workers like sweeper, water-carrier, cooker, etc. Besides these, various cottage industries are built-up and they are also related with these peripheral activities. Their activities have been largely ascribed by the religious base of the temple. Besides these, some people come to the pilgrimage place only for making a tour. They travel only for pleasure of mind, not for deity.

Their socio-economic activities are not related with the religious activities of that sacred centre. These different types of activities are defined as non-religious activities. Various transport authorities, such as railways, land transport like bus, tracker (a special type of jeep), rickshaw-pullers, etc. different garment shops, medical stores, different stationary shops, etc. are treated as non-religious agents, since their activities are not directly confined by the deity of the temple. However, the pilgrimage of the temple largely influences the economic condition of these non-religious agents. On the other hand, both non-religious and religious activities are interdependent and they both are directly or indirectly related to the Economic Culture through market. In the market, the pilgrims want to buy their religious requirements and, on the other hand, the sacred group and ritual associated people supply this particular culture to fulfill their demands. Thus, the interaction between demand and supply of these religious cultures establish a perfect relationship of Temple Culture with Economic Culture.

This relationship is explained separately by Fig.4. In this diagram, we divide cultural economics into two parts from the religious point of view. These are: (a) Religious Culture, and (b) Non-Religious Culture. The cultural activities, which are confined by the religion, are called Religious Culture. Contrarily, other cultures such as music, art, dance, archeology, etc. which are not directed by the religion, are called Non- religious Culture.

Now, the Religious Culture is again categorised into two parts. One is Temple Culture and another is Non-Temple Culture. Both these cultures are related to the Economic Culture through the market economy. The Temple Culture is accomplished in two ways. These are: (1) Religious Activities, and (2) Non-Religious Activities.

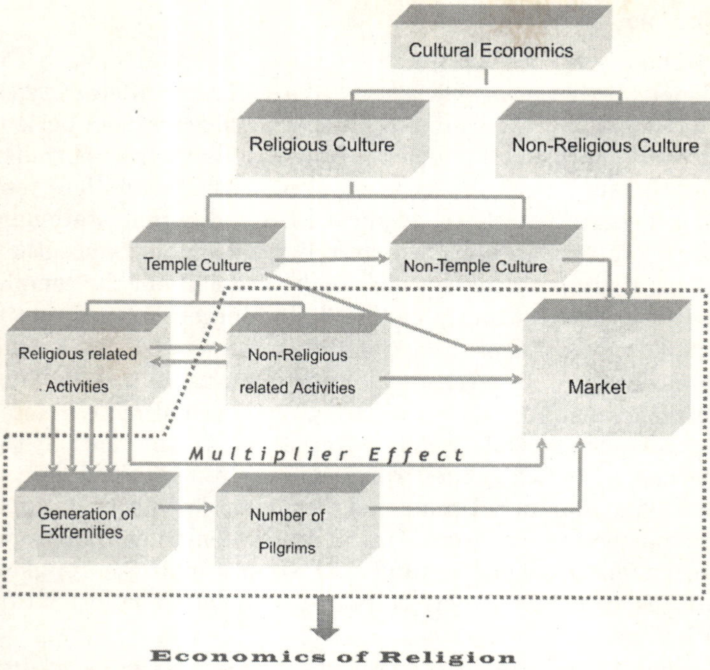

Fig. 4: Inter-relation between Temple Culture and Economic Culture.

The economic activities are defined under the religious activities by the Multiplier and External effects of the activities. Again, the economic activities are also generated by the intra-temple economic political environment among the religious practitioners.

(i) Intra-temple Economic-political Environment: It is the matter, which forecasts that there are many organisations of the beneficiary groups of cultural agents, who supply the different ritual services. Sometimes, in the critical situation, they may afforded by their organisation. The activities of those organisations are not directly related to the Economic Culture. The members of these organisations are directly related to the Economic Culture via market by the generation of multiplier and external effects.

(ii) Multiplier Effect: Various cultural agents associated with the temple and other associates under this peripheral activity earn revenues from the market to maintain their livelihood and their standard of living gradually increases due to the 'Multiplier Effect', which is manifested from the demand-supply interaction of religious practices among the religious practitioners.

(iii) External Effect: Another effect, generating from the Temple Culture, is the 'External Effect'. There are two types of externalities. One is Positive Externality, which raises the importance of the sacred centre to the pilgrims, and another is Negative Externality, which reduces the importance of this place.

Positive Externality: This effect of Temple Culture would be generated by the popular myths of the temple, transport facilities, infrastructural facilities, etc. That is, the professional narration of scriptural and mythological stories of that temple as well as God, increased advantageous means of various land transports, better infrastructure to fulfill the religious needs, etc. which increase the value of that place to the visitors. As a result, more pilgrims come to this place to fulfill their religious requirements, which better-off the economic conditions of that place.

The pilgrims, who visit a sacred place, are inspired by a wide variety of considerations surrounding consecration to the deity, personal, and pecuniary gains and so on. The purpose of visit to the pilgrimage place, by the self-fulfilling processing of the spiritual and material needs, the individual expects to earn religious merit, salvation, redemption of sin and also to get success in life and get an employment, service promotion, etc. A large percentage of pilgrims also come to this centre for the therapeutic purposes. From the generation of that self-fulfilling process, the Temple Culture creates positive externalities. Moreover, the positive externality effect is also enhanced by the influence of certain mass media like films, folk-drama, newspapers and the propagation of the gospel of god. By getting information from the devotees and other informants and by the cascading effect of such information, pilgrims got enthused to come to the religious places in large groups, which generates the positive external effects in the market.

Negative Externality: Temple Culture generates negative external effect in the market by degrading the environment, e.g., pollution. To protect the environment, the government, municipal authorities, etc. interfere into the religious activities by imposing different types of restrictions, such as taxes, different service charges, etc. This increases the cost of ritual activities, which reduces the value of the pilgrimage place and creates negative external effects in the market. Sometimes, the behaviour of the sacred specialists and other religious associates, such as asking the maximum charges for offering worship, also generates the negative external effect in the market.

Through the generation of externality and the multiplier effect in the market, Cultural Economic Bridge up the Temple Culture with the Economic Culture, which gives the incentives to the different cultural agents to maintain their livelihood and huge amount of employment is also generated from this interaction. Sometimes, Temple Culture is directly related to the Economic Culture through 'market". Temple authority earns income by renting its property like land, rooms for shops to the people for business, from interests of the liquid assets in the bank, as well as from the gifts of devotees, etc.

Besides this, the non-religious activities under Temple Culture are related to the Economic Culture through the market, as already discussed earlier.

The bounded area of the diagram (4) represents the concept of Economics of Religion, which is my area of study. In my project, we will show, how the activities of Temple Culture are built-up, based on a case study with reference to Tarakeswar in West Bengal.

1.4 Economics of Temple Culture: A Case Study with Reference to Tarakeswar

The importance of the system of religious belief of Tarakeswar and its temple is not only confined to the religious aspect, but also a similar importance can be traced into the economic aspect. In the introduction, we have already said, the economy of Tarakeswar town depends considerably on the temple of *'Taraknath'*. Now, we determine or estimate the price or worth of this Temple Culture along with the Economic Culture and the effectiveness of this culture for economic development by this project study.

The definitions of 'Religion' include: (1) a belief in something sacred, for example, God or other supernatural things on which various ritual acts are focussed, (2) it is a distinction between sacred and profane object, (3) characteristically, religion is a religious feeling like awe, sense of mystery, sense of guilty, adoration, which tend to arouse in the presence of sacred objects and during the practice of ritual, (4) it is a prayer and other forms of communication with supernatural. All these are correlated with the economic activities of the society that can be discussed on the basis of Tarakeswar.

From the perspective of belief in God *'Taraknath'* and from different ritual acts, which focus the sacred object *'Shiva Linga'*, we can say that religious culture of temple *'Taraknath'* is a creature of productive forces. It generates many economic activities. For the belief in 'God Shiva', many pilgrims come to Tarakeswar to fulfill their religious requirements, whereas the inhabitants and some people from outside help them fulfill their requirements by supplying the products necessary for *'Darshan'*. In return of supplying services to pilgrims, the providers earn income to maintain their livelihood.

From the second definition, *'Shiva Linga'* is a sacred stone, which is the sign of deity and generates more income and employment opportunities, but the profane stone does not exhibit such income and employment. Thus, the Economic Culture is defined by the Religious Culture.

The third and fourth definitions of religion reflect that virtuous people come for *'darshan'* or making a *'tirtha'* to Tarakeswer Temple to derive spiritual satisfaction, e.g., peace, adoration, joy, etc., which tend to be awakened in the presence of sacred thing. By the different ritual practices such as praying and other forms of communication with the God, pilgrims accumulate religious merit (i.e., *'puja')* and remove their sins (i.e.,*'papa')*. To acquire this, the pious people are ready to pay for it. That is, they purchase this Religious Culture from the ritual associates and the concerned individuals earn a lot by transporting necessary religious products and its various ancillaries to the pilgrims. The pilgrimage place, Tarakeswer, performs exactly these types of activities.

Therefore, by these definitions, we can say that in Tarakeswer, every economic activity is governed by the religious activities of the temple of *Taraknath*.

1.4.1 Economic Significance of Temple Culture

The temple of *Taraknath* at Tarakeswar has changed considerably the economic pattern of the town. Economic pattern depends upon the occupational structure, standard of living of the inhabitants of the town, socio-economic infrastructural conditions, etc. The occupational profile reflects that at Tarakeswer, too, a substantial portion of population earns their livelihood from the temple and its pilgrims and the nature and extent of dependency vary from one group to the other. That is, some are acquiring more from it by virtue of their ritual position or by the exclusive nature of their occupation. Through the discussion of the different occupational

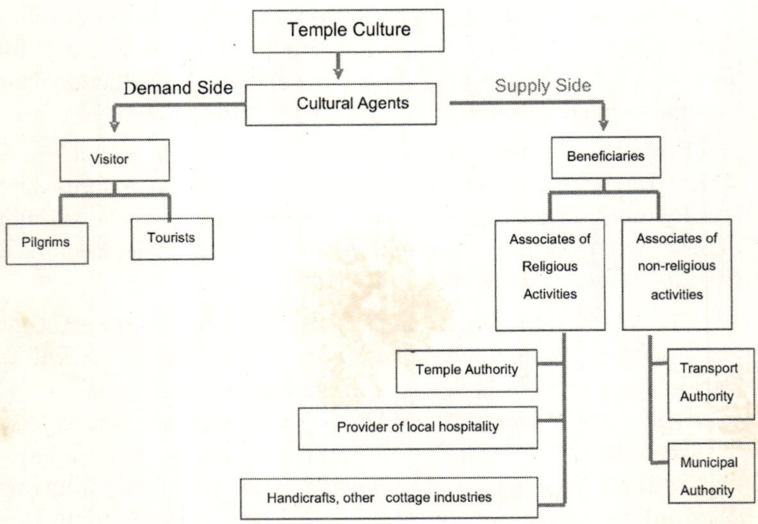

Fig. 5: Different Components of Temple Culture.

groups, who are offering some kind of religious services, we examine the economic inducement of the temple on the pattern of their activities. Temple Culture reveals that there is an economic association among different groups of cultural agents, who provide the ritual practices and its ancillaries to others, who demand it, in order to earn their subsistence. This can be represented by a schematic Fig. 5.

(a) Pilgrims: Tarakeswer has now reached the phenomenal popularity; millions of devotees come to this sacred place in long processions every year. The people, who come to this holy place to fulfill their religious desires, are called pilgrims.

We have already come to know that the need for active participation of the consumer is an important matter for the generation of productive activities under any cultural system. The active role of the consumer is evidenced in the culture of temple. In common parlance, we call the sympathisers of the religious activities as believers and others as non-believers.

At the religious centre, pilgrims mainly fall under the category of believers. In economic sense, a pilgrim is a typical consumer under the religious cultural economics. Although, the believers are not necessarily pilgrims but pilgrims are necessarily believers.

The virtuous people spend their time on visiting the holy place or worshiping the God. So, production of something is the opportunity cost of time that the pilgrim spends for pilgrimage activities. This is the production side of pilgrimage activity. On the other hand, the opportunity cost of income from or expenditure on pilgrimage activity is the consumption side of that particular culture. In this way, we can differentiate the cultural economics from the traditional economics through the concept of pilgrim.

From the study of Tarakeswar pilgrimage, thousands and thousands of virtuous people come to this sacred place for the devotion to deity, personal and pecuniary gains and so on. On some auspicious occasions such as *'Sivaratri, 'Chaitra Sankranti'* and *'Sravani Purnima'*, this number rises multiple times. These will create massive demand for ritual goods and practices at this place. By fulfilling these demands, beneficiary groups earn a lump-sum amount of income and maintain their livelihood. From this demand and supply interaction, therefore, we can estimate the cultural importance of Tarakeswar in economics.

General Information about the Pilgrims of Tarakeswar

It is difficult to estimate the number of pilgrims. But from the information of local people and transport authority, it is found that the number has been increasing continuously and appreciably during the last 15-20 years.

Classification of Pilgrims: Various types of pilgrims come to Tarakeswar throughout the year, commonly referred as *'Yatris'*. By differentiating the types of pilgrims, we get mainly three types. These are *Sada, Jal* and *Dharna.* The regular pilgrims, who come mostly by train, bus or other transport, are called *'Sada Yatris'*. *'Jal Yatris'* are those pilgrims, who bring the holy water of Ganga in pots hanging from the two ends of a yoke-pole and covering all the way on foot. They mostly come to this holy place during the period of *'Sravani'* and *'Gajan'*, i.e., in the months of July-August and March-April, respectively. According to the nature of contact with the priests, the pilgrims are also categorised into three types. These are *'Nutan Yatris', 'Alapi Yatris'* and *'Dalal Yatris'*. The pilgrims, who approach their priests directly and the priests look after them personally, are known as *'Nutan Yatris'*. *'Alapi Yatris'* comprise those pilgrims who have the clientele relationship with the priests. On the other hand, *'Dalal Yatris'* are those who are related to the priests momentary and contractually. Besides these, there are different types of pilgrims according to the purpose of their visits.

Social Characteristics: It was found from Dr P. Chakraborty's report that most of the pilgrims arrive to this pilgrimage place from different districts of West Bengal such as Midnapur, Nadia, Bankura, Birbhum, Murshidabad, North and South 24 Parganas, Burdwan, Howrah and also from the capital city of Kolkata. Very small number of pilgrims is from neighbouring states like Bihar, Odisha, etc. Bengali as well as non-Bengali pilgrims visit this place. In *'Sravani'* season, the proportion of non-Bengali pilgrims is comparably higher than any others. Maximum pilgrims, who come to this place, are from villages than from cities.

Tarakeswar is mostly visited by some common castes. For example, the *Brahmins* followed by the *'Kayasthas'*, the *'Mahisyas'*, the *'Banias'*, etc. The regular pilgrims consist of high and middle caste groups. But in the auspicious months, pilgrims arrive more from high and low caste groups.

Economic Features: Pilgrimage is an act of performance and exercise of the willingness. The economic condition, occupation, etc. play an important role in it. Many pilgrims come to this place with the poor occupational background. Pilgrims are classified into different categories according to the different sectors of the economy such as agriculture, business, service, profession, manual work, etc., which they belonged to. They purchase the ritual services according to their economic condition. On the basis of a broad assessment of their economic condition, an offhand fig. of their monthly income or expenditure gives the correct picture of the economic status of these pilgrims. Most of the regular pilgrims are engaged with services and business. The pilgrims from different professions, business, manual works, agriculture, etc., come to this place in the *'Sravani'* month. They are rational. How they are influenced by this particular culture, yet their poor economic condition can be analysed in this project study.

Demographic Features: The demographic characteristics of the pilgrims are that the *'Sravani'* pilgrims consist of the younger people. The regular and *'Gajan'* pilgrims include middle-aged and old people, respectively. From the gender classification, it is shown that the percentage of female pilgrims in the regular category being much higher than male pilgrims. But in the *'Sravani'* and *'Gajan'*, the male pilgrims in all age-groups are relatively higher than the female pilgrims. Also from the marital status, more than 80 per cent of the pilgrims are married. Very little percentage of the pilgrims consists of widowed and divorced people. Moreover, maximum unmarried pilgrims are found in *'Sravani'*.

However, with these distinct characteristics, many virtuous people come to this place and purchase this religious service with the exchange of their income to fulfill their ritual satisfaction, which is the important provision of the people associated with the culture to maintain their livelihood.

(b) Tourists: Tourists are those people who make their trip for pleasure, not for any ritual activities. Since Tarakeswar is a pilgrimage place, so a very small number of tourists come to this place in comparison to the pilgrims. They also consume the amenities from the local hospitality providers, which generate the economic activities.

From the supply side, the demands of the visitors are fulfilled by the various types of beneficiaries. The beneficiary groups of Cultural Agents are divided into two categories: (1) the group associated with religious activities, and (2) the group associated with non-religious activities.

Associates of Religious Activities: These are the people who supply the religious services to the pilgrims. These associates are classified into three groups: (1) Temple authority, (2) Provider of local hospitality, and (3) Handicraft and other cottage industries.

(1) Temple Authority: In Tarakeswar, religious functions and the administration of the temple of Taraknath are directed by the Temple Authority. This can be explained by the Fig. 6.

According to the activity and the associates, the temple authority is divided into two parts: (a) Temple employees, who undertake all the ritual activities and administer the temple activities, and (b) Temple itself, which reflects the own activities of the temple, such as collection of different types of taxes, interests, gifts from the devotees, etc. and provide various developmental services and amenities to the pilgrims.

(a) Temple Employees: Temple employees are also categorised into two groups; (1) Sacred Group, who are doing the diverse ritual roles and functionaries. This Sacred Group is also divided into two parts.

Firstly, *'Mohanta'* is the head of the monastery of Tarakeswar. As an employee of the estate authority of temple, he draws a fixed monthly salary. Besides this, he gets usual allowance for annual pilgrimage and free boarding and lodging. *'Mohanta'* is a the religious head, so his economic interaction with the other economic groups is very little. To run the estate administration and management, he has to employ accountant, manager, cashier, surveyors and other manual workers. Since *'Mohanta'* is rearing an austere austerities, i.e., a saint, so, most of his income is spent in philanthropic and religious matters.

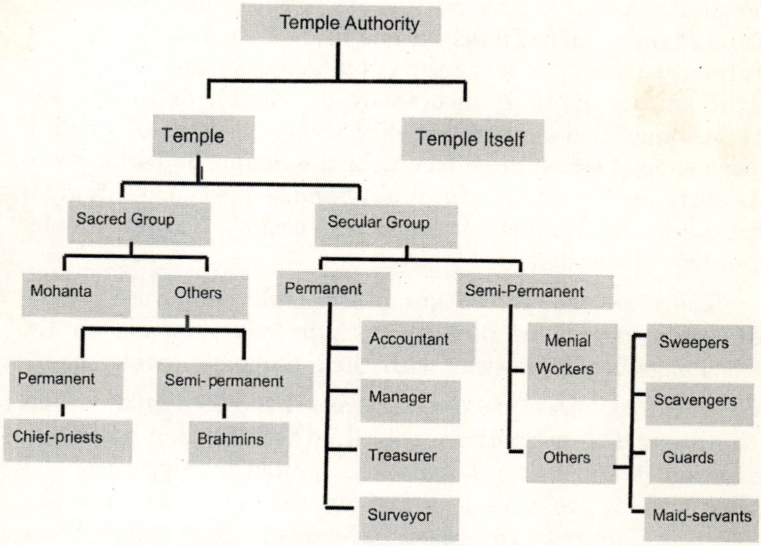

Fig. 6: Different Agents of Temple Authority.

The second category is 'others', which is divided into two sub-categories.

(a) Permanent Employees: They draw a fixed salary from the estate. At Tarakeswar, the Temple Estate has one chief priest, who draws a fixed monthly salary along with free boarding and lodging from the estate. Moreover, they get regular income in the form of gifts of their disciples. They also earn a lump-sum amount of income from the narration of religious and mythological stories in different places more than once in a month. With the daily ritual practices in the temple, they also recite the scriptural and mythological stories on certain religious occasions at this pilgrimage centre.

(b) Semi-permanent Employees: They are recruited as per the requirement. In the temple estate, there are five Brahmin teachers who teach in the Sanskrit College. They also direct certain ritual practices in the temple of Taraknath and other Gods. They recite from the holy books during the worship. They get a fixed monthly salary, free boarding and lodging from the estate. They have also a number of other sources of income. Some of them have cultivated land at their home. From which they get a share of the crops. Beside this, some of them earn a fixed income from their disciples outside Tarakeswar, by officiating the ritual activities and also earn a lump-sum amount of income by practising astrology and prescribing stones in the jewellry shops in Kolkata. Another has a shop of consecrated food near the temple at Tarakeswar. As shrine priests, these Brahmin *pundits* also earn a regular income by assisting their clients who come to Tarakeswar for *darshan* of the deity.

Therefore, the sacred group of temple employees, except '*Mohanta*', somehow directly or indirectly depends on the pilgrimage of Tarakeswar with their economic involvement.

Another group of temple employees is the (2) Secular Group. This group does not perform any ritual activities but it depends upon on it and also related with the deity activities of this pilgrimage centre. Like sacred group, the secular group is also categorised into two groups: (1) Permanent Group and (2) Semi-permanent Group.

(1) Under permanent temple employees, there are one manager, one accountant, one cashier and some clerks and surveyors. They receive salary on regular basis, paid in cash from the estate authority. Various types of official works such as accounts, tax collection, planning, survey, maintaining treasures, etc. and all administrative activities are exercised by them.

(2) Under the second category, i.e., the Semi-permanent employees, come two groups of workers; (a) menial workers and (b) operators.

The menial workers such as sweepers, scavengers, guides and maid-servants receive either some fixed amount of food grains or some payments in cash and kind. The major proportion of the paid employees have nominal education, have no experience and that's why their remuneration would be meagre. So, they use to make a private earning through corrupt means.

Another group of semi-permanent employees is operators. They are occasionally employed, e.g., the people, who supply the drinking water from the estate water tank, look after the treatment of sacred pond *'Dudh pukur'* by the pilgrims, etc. Like menial workers, they also get minimum income. Besides the earning from the estate, they also have a good earning from the wealthy disciples in the form of gifts.

To examine the economic importance of the religious estate, the employees have been analysed in terms of their area of origin. It is found that more than 50 per cent of the total temple employees come from the local area of Tarakeswar. So, there is a preponderance of local people among the employees. But the economic position is better for the regional employees who come from outside of Tarakeswar, but from within the district Hooghly than the local and supra-regional employees. Due to their higher academic qualifications, they hold the higher salaried posts.

Again, the economic imbalance is also created due to the caste diversification at this sacred centre. The maximum patronage has been enjoyed by the local higher caste people. Although the middle caste employees get income, which is some better off than the low caste employees.

So, at this pilgrimage place, the economic structure of the temple employees is amalgamating with their social structure.

The religious institution of Taraknath has pronounced secular activities in the economic sphere. This can be shown in Fig. 6.

(c) Temple Itself: Another part of temple authority, where we discuss the temple's own activities for the pilgrimage. Temple authority provides different types of services and amenities to the pilgrims for their better ritual practices. For example, to worship the God *'Taraknath'*, to take bath in the sacred pond *'Dudh pukur'*, the temple authority gives different types of hospitalities. Besides, providing benefits to the devotees, the temple authority itself enhances the religious image of this place, and also donates for various charitable and relief purposes for the welfare of the people at Tarakeswar. Moreover, the temple authority itself arranges places for parking the vehicles of the pilgrims in the estate ground. Again, temple authority prepares sacred food in the temple to feed the pilgrims twice a day. This ritual is called *'bhandara'*. In the auspicious season such as in *'Sravani'*, the temple authority arranges a special system, by which many pilgrims pour the sacred water of *'Ganga'* on the sacred stone, *'Shiva Linga'* at a time. In this auspicious season, the temple authority also arranges to stay the pilgrims in the temple premises. In order to provide these hospitalities and amenities to the pilgrims, the temple authority does some expenses. In order to maintain different expenses, the temple authority earns itself in different way. It can be represented by Fig.7.

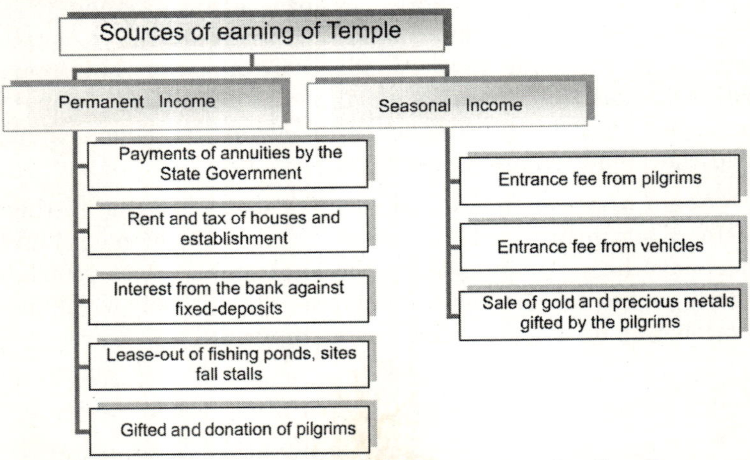

Fig. 7: Different Sources of Earnings of the Temple.

The earning of the temple is divided into two categories: (a) Permanent Income and (b) Seasonal Income.

(a) Permanent Income: By the permanent income of the temple, we mean the regular income, obtained by the temple authority from different sources. In Fig. 7, the permanent income of the temple authority obtained from five different sources is shown. Firstly, a fixed sum of money or allowances paid yearly by the State Government to the temple authority. Secondly, from the gifts and donations from the pilgrims, the temple authority earns a lump-sum amount of income and also from the investment of these funds in the bank as fixed deposit; temple authority earns interests from these deposits. This is the third source of permanent income of the temple. Fourthly, by keeping houses and other establishment, the estate authority earns a lot in the form of rent and tax. Finally, by leasing-out fishing ponds, tonsuring centre, sites for stalls through auctioning, the temple authority earns income.

(b) Seasonal Income: Besides these permanent incomes, the temple authority also earns a large amount of income seasonally. It collects taxes through coupon as a parking charge from the vehicles by which the pilgrims come to this sacred place. Especially at the time of *'Sravani'*, the temple authority also collects entrance fees as service charge through coupon from every pilgrim. Occasionally, by selling gold and precious metals, which are denoted by the wealthy pilgrims, the temple authority collects money.

Therefore, the people under temple authority depend upon this economic involvement of the temple to maintain their livelihood.

(2) Local Hospitality Providers: Another associate of the beneficiary group of cultural agent is local hospitality providers. This group confers services to pilgrims to mitigate their religious requirements. They supply different types of amenities and assist the ritual worships and rites to the devotees.

The local hospitality providers are divided into two sub-groups. These are (1) Sacred Group, which works in the religious complex for assisting the pilgrims to fulfill their ritual demands, and (2) Secular Group, which supplies various types of conveniences and opportunities to the pilgrims to accomplish their religious as well as personal demands. The classification of these providers is represented by Fig. 8.

In this Fig., the Sacred Group is also divided into two parts: (1) Pilgrim Guides and (2) Private Priests. They are sacred specialists for their particular function. Pilgrim guides are a group of religious associates who work as middle-men between the pilgrims and the priests and bridge-up them by creating an economic relationship. Pilgrim guides are found at the railway station, bus stop or on the main road leading to the temple of *'Taraknath',* waiting eagerly for catching up with the pilgrims. In this figure (8), there are three types of pilgrim guides, (a) *'regular'*, (b) *'casual'* and (c) *'seasonal'*. Regular pilgrim guides do this job on permanent basis for earning their livelihood. More than 45 per cent people are engaged with this category. The second category consists of casual pilgrims. They have a permanent occupation elsewhere other than this pilgrim-hunting. The casual pilgrim guides do this job mainly on holidays and during festive seasons or on someone's behalf. Approximately 50 per cent of people are engaged under this second category. And the third category consists of seasonal pilgrim guides, who work during the festive seasons, such as on *'Sivaratri', 'Chaitra-Sankranti'* and *'Sravani Purnima',* once or twice in a year for a few days only. The regular and casual pilgrim guides are local people and most of the pilgrim guides are Brahmins. On the other hand, the seasonal guides come from the neighbouring villages and some of them come from other castes like *'Sadgop', 'Tamli', 'Mahishya',* etc. The pilgrim guides earn a large amount of income from pilgrims by escorting them to the right priest and also by preparing different arrangements for a convenient accommodation, quick entrance of the pilgrims into the temple and also to worship 'God' and so on. Most of the pilgrim guides, among the regular pilgrim guides, that is, more than 70 per cent of them are doing this job on contractual basis with the priests and the owners of the rest houses. The guides are given a lump-sum amount of income as advances for supplying those pilgrims every year. Besides these monetary assistances, different types of help such as crops, clothing, etc. are given to pilgrim guides by the priests and rest-house owners. Sometimes, the guides are also remunerated for doing farm and domestic works in their houses.

By the pilgrim hunting, the pilgrim guides earn a large amount of income to maintain their livelihood. They also depend largely on the gifts, which are collected from the pilgrims for subsistence. They usually earn Rs 200-300 per day. The economic dependency of the regular pilgrim guides on the pilgrim hunting is much more than that of the casual and seasonal pilgrim guides. Because the former have no other alternative sources of income, except the pilgrim hunting, whereas the latter two categories have other sources of income in addition to this work. They are employed in other sectors of economy, such as in agriculture, services and business or as artisans elsewhere. Since the pilgrim guides are largely dependent on the intensity of pilgrims, so their economic activities and behaviour are largely guided by the pilgrimage of this sacred centre.

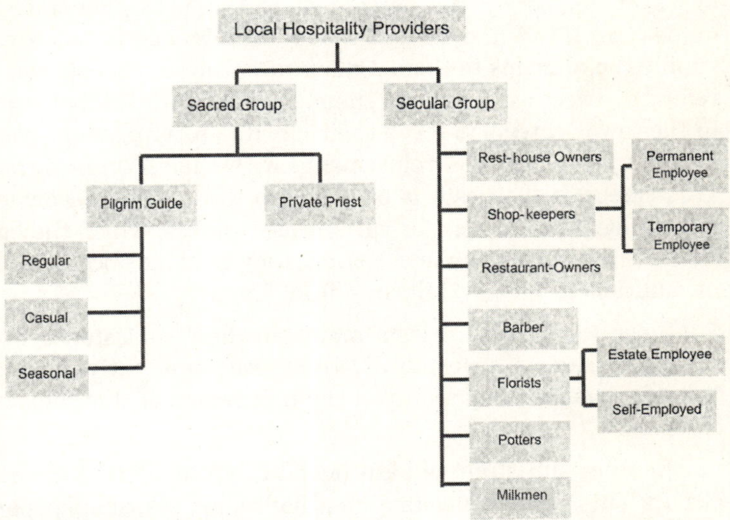

Fig. 8: Different Components of Local Hospitality Group.

Now, another category of the sacred group is private priests. They work in the religious complex of Tarakeswar. By assisting in ritual worships and the rites of the devotee, they earn their livelihood. There are 160 private priests. This number excludes the chief priest, who is a permanent employee of the temple authority. There are a number of factors on which the earning of a priest depends. These are the availability of pilgrims and their types and desires, auspicious nature of the day, business relationships with the other associates such as pilgrim guides, owners of the rest houses and so on. Besides priest-craft, some of them earn a lot of income by conducting different types of sacred ceremonies like *'Annaprason'*, *'Upanayan'*, etc., to their clients. Other additional sources of their income include agriculture, business, renting houses, etc.

In Tarakeswar, there are different categories of priests. The priests belonging to the upper category maintain *'jajmani'* relationship with the *'Alapi Yatris'*, i.e., they maintain traditional clientele relationship with the pilgrims. The middle category of priests maintains clientele relationship with the *'Dalal Yatris'*, which is mainly transitory in nature. These priests keep a contractual tie-up with the pilgrim guides. They are also helped by the owners of rest houses. The pilgrim guides are hired and offered money in advance to catch and supply the pilgrims to them. Sometimes, the rest house owners refer the excess pilgrims to them. And the priests, belonging to the lower category, serve their clients on contractual basis. They have no clientele relationship with their *'Nutan Yatris'*. This category of priests is obedient to the rest house owners to get pilgrims and also for various assistances, which they get from them. During the lean period, they get loans occasionally in addition to getting pilgrims from them.

Since the private priests maintain their subsistence from the profession of priest-craft, their economic activities and behaviour mostly depend upon the pilgrimage of this religious complex.

Another sub-group of local hospitality providers is Secular Group. This group consists of rest house owners, shopkeepers, restaurant owners, barbers, florists, water carriers, milk men, potters, etc., as shown in Fig. 8.

There are many (more than 70) rest houses at Tarakerwar, which provide different types of facilities to devotees to fulfill their religious requirements. These are mainly owned by the private sector. But there are few rest houses owned by some charitable trusts and two guest houses owned by the municipal authority. Some owners are from local areas and some others are immigrants from outside of Tarakerwar.

By providing various amenities to the pilgrims, the rest house owners earn a large amount of income for their subsistence. These earnings depend upon several factors, such as the flow of pilgrims to Tarakeswar, economic condition of the pilgrims, the number of rooms available for rent, etc. There are different categories of rest houses here. These are *'pucca'* and *'kutcha'* houses. The *'pucca'* houses have the facilities of bathroom, toilet, fan, etc., which attract the wealthy clients. But the poor pilgrims want to stay in the *'kutcha'* houses, because they have no enough money to purchase the comfort.

Again, the rest house owners earn more income if they have more number of rooms available for rent. Some rest houses have the sitting facilities for the priests and the pilgrim guides for getting a steady supply of pilgrims. Some rest houses possess the shops for selling sweetmeat, ritual articles, etc. needed by the pilgrims. The convenient location of rest houses that are situated near the temple is also a factor for enhancing income. Some of the owners also earn income from other sources such as agricultural land and other commercial activities.

The rest house owners under upper category, who possess *'pucca'* houses that are situated in a vintage position, have contacts with a large number of priests and pilgrim guides for getting more pilgrims. Some of them, who are *Brahmins*, serve as shine priests. Again some of them earn income by doing work as clerk, stenographer, teacher, etc. But the infra-structural arrangements of the rest houses under lower category are not so cherishing hope. So, the rest houses owners under lower and lower middle categories generally fail to procure more pilgrims. Sometimes, they earn income by doing the services as storekeepers, care-takers, retail shop assistants, etc. outside the area. The rest house owners under middle category have no cultivable land and the source of income is limited for them. Besides the usual share from the pilgrim guides, they earn some money by putting out to hire the bedrolls, utensils and other mundane articles to the devotees.

Sometimes, the rest house owners generate different types of employment opportunities in the society. They employ some persons to make a special type of sweetmeat needed for ritual, offering to god and also recruit some maid servants to look after the customer pilgrims of the rest houses.

In this way, by providing the various hospitalities to the pilgrims, the rest house owners maintain their subsistence.

Another sub-group of the local secular group is of shopkeepers. There are two types of shopkeepers. One, who have permanent stalls, and the other, who have temporary stalls. Some people from inside and outside of Tarakeswar do their business by hiring the stalls from estate authority and municipality. These are the permanent stalls for fixed hiring periods. But in the auspicious seasons, some people emigrate from different districts to Tarakeswar for business and hire stalls on temporary basis. Sometimes, in the festive seasons, the shopkeepers set-up temporary stalls in front of their main shops and display the commodities.

Most of the shops around the temple mainly sell the ritual articles for the pilgrims. With these shops, there are many other shops which sell the essential commodities in order to fulfill the daily needs of the inhabitants. Therefore, the earning of their livelihood largely depends upon the inflow of pilgrims to this pilgrimage place, Tarakeswar.

Similarly, another sub-category of the secular group is that of the restaurant owners. Many pilgrims come to this sacred centre every day. Most of them use various restaurants to satisfy their hunger. There are many restaurants, which earn a lump-sum amount of money by selling food items to the pilgrims and other people. The economic activities of restaurant owners are similar to those of the rest house owners. The restaurant owners also create employment at that place like the rest house owners; and they earn a good income like the rest house owners and shopkeepers.

In the festive seasons, for three or four months in a year, they all make a very good income which is suffice to make them free from any debt, and some savings are also made, which they fall back upon, when the pilgrimage seasons are over. For that reason, all the local hospitality providers eagerly await for the pilgrimage seasons.

Besides these ritual associates, there are some other sub-groups of secular category, such as barbers, florists, potters, water carriers, milkmen, etc. who are directly linked with this sacred zone. They all earn their livelihood by providing goods and services to pilgrims and also from other ritual purposes.

At Tarakeswar, both Bengali and non-Bengali barbers have been working for four to five generations. They work at the tonsuring centre, under the supervision of head barber, on a co-operative basis, who takes the annual lease from the estate authority. Besides this, it is obligatory for every barber to serve various types of functionaries of the temple as well as sacred centre, such as washing the floor of the temple, cleaning the deity's utensils, carrying the ritual articles from the central store to the temple kitchen, etc. by rotation. In lieu of these services, they get midday meal from the central kitchen and consecrated food as refreshment. Among them, one of the barbers washes the feet of the religious head daily, when he visits the temple. Again, they provide the tonsorial services to the teachers, students and the employees of the Sanskrit Institution. By doing tonsorial work, they get some remunerations. They also collect fees for tonsuring from the the pilgrims and other people. They also earn some additional income through the patronage of priests, pilgrim guides, rest house owners, etc. They also get grants in the form of grains, clothing, and money by providing services at the houses of the priests and the rest house owners, etc. Due to the meagre income and poor economic condition and extreme poverty, some of the Bengali barbers do the tonsorial work in the houses of local people to earn some additional income. Moreover, in the leisure time, the non-Bengali group of barbers is found working at the different saloons at Tarakeswar.

The florists are categorised into two sub-categories. These are: (1) Estate employed *'Mali'* and (2) Self-employed florists. The five estate employed florists get monthly salary by supplying flowers daily to the temple from the estate garden. The second group of florists is self-employed, who sell flowers, garlands, *'vilwa'* leaves and small earthen vessels, filled with the water of 'Ganga' and raw milk to the pilgrims on the bank of sacred pond *'Dudh Pukur'*. With selling these articles, some of them put sectarian mark *'tilak'* on the forehead of the pilgrims. Besides these, they also keep in custody the cloths and garments of the pilgrims, who take bathe.

Like the barbers, the florists also do their business on co-operative basis. They have formed co-operatives with the pottery dealers, sacred water dealers and milkmen. By their co-operation, the florists prepare the decorated small earthen vessels with white flowers, garlands, *'vilwa'* leaves, filled with the water of 'Ganga' and raw milk and sell it to the pilgrims. From the earning of selling these articles, the florists give share to the potters, water carriers, milkmen, and the rest of the income is enjoyed by the florists themselves. By doing this work, they earn their subsistence.

Water carriers are another sub-group of secular hospitality providers. They are appointed by estate to supply the water of 'Ganga' from Sheoraphuli to the temple. They are doing their work hereditarily. They also sell the water to the florists for the preparation of sacred *'Jal-Ghat'*. They earn some steady income from the estate authority and also from the florists on co-operative basis.

Among the familial industries, the pottery comprises another sub-group of secular providers. The maximum demand is generated from the owners of tea-stalls, sweetmeat dealers, local households, dealers of different ritual articles, florists, etc. At Tarakeswar, there are many Bengali and Bihari engaged with these activities. Very small number of Bengali potters is engaged in this work for full time basis. Most of them do agricultural operation, goldsmith, photography, painting, petty trade and so on, rather pottery making. They also search for jobs like day labour, hawking, etc. The economic dependence of the Bengali potters upon the pilgrimage centre is less compared to the non-Bengali potters; most of them are involved with this craft. They remain busy throughout the year for making earthen vessel named *'Jal-ghat'*, earthen cup named *'Khuri'*, *'Sara'*, *'Malsha'*, etc. and sell them to the tea stalls, sweetmeat shops, hotels, rest houses, florists, etc., with whom the potters fix their contracts. In this way, they earn their livelihood.

The potters sometimes, especially during the festive seasons, generate employment at Tarakeswar. They recruit labourers to operate the stone wheels manually. For this, the potters give them remunerations, and also free food and lodging.

To worship the God *Taraknath*, milk is an important ritual article which is supplied by the milkmen, who are another sub-group of the secular category. The estate authority has employed some milkmen to supply the milk for the temple ritual from the estate's cowshed to the temple. For doing this, they are remunerated steadily along with food from the central kitchen.

They also sell milk to the various tea stalls, sweetmeat shops, and households on contractual basis and also supply it to florists on co-operative basis. These businesses are also being done by the outside milkmen. By doing this business, they earn their livelihood.

In this way, by providing different types of goods and services to the temple as well as to the pilgrims, the local hospitality providers earn income for their subsistence and also generate some sort of employment.

(3) Handicrafts and other Cottage Industries: The cult of *Taraknath* helps develop a number of handicrafts and cottage industries in the neighbouring areas at Tarakeswar. This is another sub-group of beneficiaries, which is associated with the religious activities. Different types of handicrafts and cottage industries are differentiated according their origin of production as shown in Fig.9.

Some cottage industries are established in the neighbouring areas at Tarakeswar, which are called local cottage industries. These are clay pot making industries, small cotton industries, different fruit pickle making industries, armlet making industries, manufacturers of portraits of different Gods, etc. Also there are some other industries, which are situated outside Tarakeswar. Conch shell industry, metal and stone image making industry, reticulated sling making industry, yoke-pole industry, pottery industry, manufacturers of plastic clay image; all are those regional cottage industries where many people are engaged. Those, who are engaged with these industries, are living away far from Tarakeswar but obtain economic benefits from the pilgrimage activities of that place.

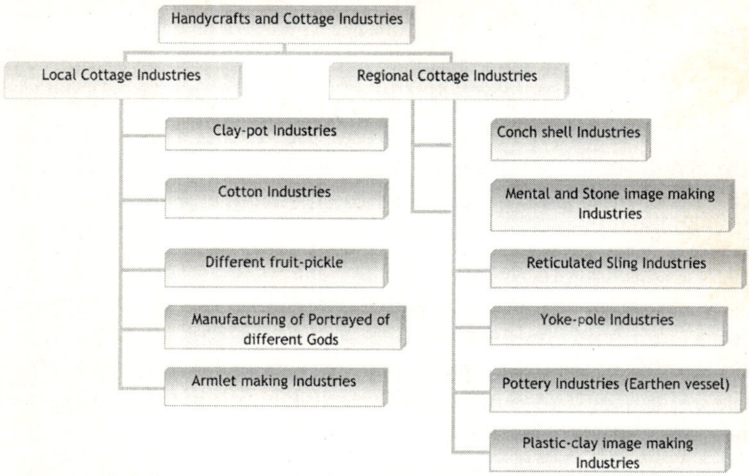

Fig. 9: Different Types of Handicrafts and Cottage Industries.

Under local cottage industries, there are a number of cotton industries which produce different types of clothes to cater to the demand of the inhabitants and the pilgrims of Tarakeswar. Especially during the festive seasons, they earn a lump-sum amount of income. The potter families supply the clay-pots to different tea stalls, restaurants, sweetmeat shops, etc. They also hire labourers to work on the potter-wheels. At this sacred place, the preparation of different fruit pickles is also an important . There are many people who are engaged in this cottage industry. On the both sides of the main road and the lanes leading to the temple, there are many shops which sell the various fruit-pickles to the pilgrims and other people and earn their livelihood. They purchase fruits from the fruit sellers in order to produce it. So, this industry is a source of income for these groups of people. From different stationary shops, some people selling the frame, boarded with wood, of photographs of different gods and earn their subsistence. Some local people are engaged in making the armlets, which are used as ritual articles at the time of worship of God *Taraknath*. These armlets are made of cotton. Many household families are engaged with this industry and earn their livelihood.

On the other hand, under the regional cottage industries,

the first place is taken by conch-shell industry. People from Barrackpore, Sheoraphuli, etc. come to this place to sell the articles made by conch. On the festive occasions, these producers emigrate from different places to Tarakeswar to sell conch-shell products and stay here for one or two months for their business. From this handicraft, many people maintain their livelihood. Besides this, some people come to this place with the metal and stone images of different gods to sell. Many hired labourers are engaged in both these industries. Another type of regional cottage industry is reticulated sling making industry. The families, living in Sheoraphuli and the areas around the *Nimaitirtha Ghat*, used to make the reticulated sling by jute and cotton, the creeper and nylon. By selling their product directly to the pilgrims or to the local dealers at wholesale rates, these families earn their livelihood. More than 100 workers are engaged in this industry. The income of these workers increases five to six times during the festive seasons in comparison to the lean periods through this business. Side by side with the manufacture of reticulated sling, the yoke-pole industry, pottery industry, making of earthen vessels have been developed at Sheoraphuli, outside Tarakeswar, for catering to the ritual needs of the pilgrims. More than 50 households are engaged in these crafts. Different labourers, including teenaged boys, are working in these industries on nominal wages. Besides these, the potters of Uluberia in the district of Howrah, Diamond Harbour in the district of South 24 Parganas, sell plastic clay images made by the clayed soil (*entel mati*) to the pilgrims at this pilgrimage place. Moreover, temporary stalls of jingle bells, incense sticks, flowers, and other decorative articles which are required by the pilgrims, piping-up here and there at and outside Tarakeswar, from which many people maintain their subsistence. Since hundreds of people of various ages and diverse socio-economic backgrounds are found to be engaged in different cottage industries during the pilgrim seasons. So, it generates a huge amount of employment inside as well as outside Tarakeswar.

Another group of beneficiaries, which is associated with non-religious activities at Tarakeswar, is divided into two sub-groups. These are: (1) Transport Authority; and (2) Municipal Authority.

(1) Transport Authority: For a long time, Tarakeswar has attracted many people from diverse areas. In the auspicious months and days, millions of pilgrims congregate here from near and far away places. It is difficult to estimate the numbers of pilgrims. They come to this place mainly using by various land transport systems. Transport authority is divided into groups. One is owned by the private sector and the other is owned by the government. These are two sources that have been explored to obtain figs. in this regard. This can be explained by Fig. 10.

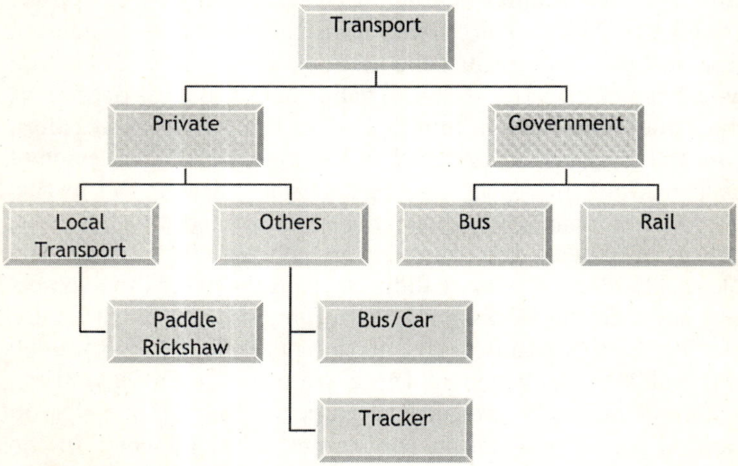

Fig. 10: Different Components of Transport Authority.

(a) Private Transport: Private transport system is categorised into sub-categories. These are local transport and others. By the first category, we mean that transport, which is locally accessible, i.e., by which we can't cover the long distances, e.g., paddle rickshaw. And under the second category, we consider those transports by which we can cover the long distances, e.g., bus, car, tracker (a special type of jeep). Mainly local people and small numbers of pilgrims come to the temple from station and other nearby places by paddle rickshaw. But many pilgrims from distant places come here by buses, cars or trackers. At Tarakeswar, there is only one bus terminus near the station. A number of local buses, express buses, private cars, trackers arrive at and depart from this terminus.

Many people associated with these various transports maintain their livelihood by escorting the local pilgrims to the temple. In the festive season, the number of land transports increases. Besides these, many pilgrims visit this place by their private or hired buses or cars. They park their vehicles in the estate ground. Moreover, many devotees come to this place on foot. They are called *'Jal Yatris'*. In *'Sravani'* and *'Gajan'*, many pilgrims wearing ochre-coloured cloths, shirts and vests, bringing holy water of 'Ganga' in the pots slung at the two ends of a yoke pole, reach there covering all the way from Sheoraphuli *Nimaitirtha Ghat* to Tarakeswar on foot.

(b) Government Transport: To access this pilgrimage centre, there are two types of government transports. One is government bus transport and another is railway transport. Pilgrims from other states, distant districts come to Tarakeswar by state buses or trains. Many 'regular' pilgrims come to Tarakeswar by rail from the capital city of Kolkata and also from different districts like Burdwan, Birbhum, Nadia, North and South 24 Parganas, etc.

The statistical data of Eastern Railway, derived from Railway Authority, Howrah Division and different private buses, trackers from their association, reveal that the visiting tendency of the tonsure pilgrims is gradually increasing day-by-day. Especially in the auspicious seasons like *'Sravani', 'Shivaratri'* and *'Chaitra Sankranti'*, the number of pilgrim passengers increases multiple times. Also on every Sunday, Monday and other usual holidays, the number of pilgrims exceeds the average. For that reason, the railways has started a special train from Howrah to Tarakeswar on every Monday for the convenience of the pilgrims. Beside this, the railways is working on a project for double line from Howrah to Nalikul and to extend the single line from Tarakeswar to Bankura. These activities will raise the socio-economic importance of that pilgrimage place.

The development of railway and road transports will provide more opportunities to the pilgrims to mitigate their ritual requirements. By providing the services to these pilgrims, the various land transports earn a lump-sum amount of income. By providing transport services, the government earns a lump-sum amount of revenue, especially during the auspicious seasons. From the past, the number of buses, trucks, etc., has increased more than one times. That would raise the employment opportunities as well as income, and will enhance the economic development of this place. These transport authorities also help for trading different agricultural goods to different places. So, transport is an indispensable factor for economic development.

(2) Municipal Authority: Another hand of the non-ritual associates of beneficiary group is Municipal Authority. The law and administration of Tarakeswar town is controlled by this authority. It comprises a chairman, cashier, accountant, auditor, clerk and other menial workers. They all get fixed salary from the government. The municipal authority provides various types of services and amenities to the inhabitants of this town. It takes a special care for providing the different types of facilities and comforts to the pilgrims to cater to their religious needs. For these services, the municipality collects different taxes from the inhabitant families. It also collects the ritual taxes from the pilgrims and parking charges from these pilgrims' vehicles. The ritual taxes are from every pilgrim only on *'Sravani'*. These ritual taxes are 50 per cent income of the earning of the estate authority that they collect by selling coupons to every pilgrim for their ritual formalities. The amount of taxes, collected from the ritual based areas surrounding the temple, is much higher than the tax obtained from the outside areas. It reflects that there exists a significant impact of temple culture on the economic condition of the municipal corporation. That's why, the municipal corporation develops and modernises the town Tarakeswar and also provides more comforts and amenities to pilgrims to attract them for visiting this place.

Therefore, like every pilgrimage place the municipal authority earns a large amount of income from this sacred centre of Tarakeswar.

From the above discussion, we can say that a wide stretch of surrounding areas of Tarakeswar comprises economically, culturally and socially linked with the towns their feeding centre. People from the various areas visit this ritual town regularly in connection with their own profession, service, education, entertainment and religious purposes. The *'cult of Taraknath'* represents the socio-economic connection of this town with the pilgrimage activities.

So, the economic network of Tarakeswar has manifold aspects involving a large area, which is defined by the Temple Culture. Therefore, it needed a detailed discussion to ascertain the categories, who are involved in maintaining their livelihood from the inflow of pilgrims, i.e., the economy of Tarakeswar is defined by the Temple Culture that is pilgrimage of this place.

1.5 Plan of the Study

The discussion of our study could be presented in eight consecutive chapters. Chapter 1 discusses the Temple Culture along with Social, Economical, Religious and Political Cultures. In this chapter, we give the various definitions, historical role of Religious Culture and also discuss the interactions of this new dimension with the other cultures. All these interactions among different cultures are illustrated on the sacred place of Tarakeswar in India.

In the second chapter, we give some descriptions about economics of religion, where we discuss definition, historical role of religious establishment and economic appearance of religion.

In the third chapter, we have briefly reviewed different works that have been done and the conclusions that have been drawn by various research works regarding the effectiveness of religious factors for economic development.

Chapter 4 gives a brief description of database for our empirical analysis. In our study, we use both primary data and secondary data in order to examine the effect of various religious ingredients on Economic Culture at Tarakeswar. And in this chapter, we also discuss about various methodologies to analyse the database.

In this fifth chapter, we first introduce the micro-level analysis of the Temple Culture. Here, we make a micro-level discussion on the pilgrims, who are the consumers of this particular culture and also on the sacred and secular (non-sacred) local hospitality providers, who supply this culture. It also attempt to explore the socio-economic profile of the pilgrims, on one hand, and we also illuminate the socio-economic dependency of the sacred groups, on the other hand.

In chapter 6, we discuss how the flow of pilgrims to any place is strictly determined by the pilgrim's valuation of the religious site. Here we are trying to quantify this mysterious phenomenon, by utilising some easily accessible known variable, 'frequency of visits' by the pilgrims to this sacred centre. We then try to relate it with a broader set of socio-economic variables. To do this, we collect primary data from the pilgrims regarding their socio-economic structure and also their intension to visit this sacred place. To analyse this information, we employ count regression model. In this chapter, we however try to understand the interaction between the local hospitality providers and the devotees through a simple simulation study.

In chapter 7, we discuss how the cultural activities generate the livelihood opportunities through demand and supply interaction of semi-skilled and unskilled workers in an urban unit. Here we examine the socio-economic characteristics of both secular and sacred hospitality providers like priests, pilgrim guides, various shopkeepers, rest house owners, etc. to show the economic dependency on religious component at the sacred centre of Tarakeswar, by using various types of statistical techniques like Tobit regression, Multiple regression, etc.

Finally, the conclusion and the findings obtained from every chapter and the corresponding remedial measures are discussed in chapter 8. In this way, we construct the entire research project to analyse 'The Economics of Temple Culture' at this sacred centre, Tarakeswar.

Before delving into our study, we first concentrate on some conceptual ideas and available literature in this regard in next two consecutive chapters. A study of economic activities of the Temple Culture and the existing literature will set the arena for our analysis. The strength as well as frailties of the existing studies are the main powerhouse behind our analytical study.

Note

1. There has been a lot of discussion regarding the relationship between religion and economic decision-making. For example see Iannaconce (1988, 1990, 1991). Deheija and Deheija (1993), Munger (2006), James and Sharpe (2007), Desender, Castro and Escamillade León (2011).

2

The Economics of Temple Culture: A Short Introduction

2.1 Introduction

Economists have always been engaged in the study of religion as an important force that shapes and re-directs the economic activity. In his famous treatise *'Arthasastra'*, Kautilya emphasises several ways through which a ruler may be able to increase the earning by fanning the religious mentality of the masses. Aristotle gave importance to the ethical considerations of political and economic activity.

Adam Smith, the father of economics, dealt with several aspects of religion in his *Wealth of Nations*. However, the discipline of economics of religion is of recent origin. It was mainly the workshop Iannaccone (1992), Kuran (2004), Barro and McCleary (2003) that really led to the birth of the economics of religion. The institutional economics developed by Douglass North (2005) also has important bearing on the development of the subject. These literatures are reviewed in the later chapter. In this chapter, we try to understand the basic ingredients of the economics of religion and its main super structures.

The chapter is divided into six sections. In section 2.2, we give some descriptions about economics of religion. Under this section, we discuss definition, historical role of religious establishment and economic appearance of religion. Here, we also light up on the importance of the system of religious belief of Tarakeswar and its temple, which can be traced into the economic aspect.

2.2 Descriptions

2.2.1 Definition

The relation between Economic Culture and Religious Culture, i.e., the economic study of religious culture, comprises a variety of sub-fields, which collectively embrace all the aspects of the socio-scientific study of religion, known as the 'Economics of Religion'. The 'Economics of Religion' is a study that seeks to explain the religious behaviour from an economic (or 'rational choice') perspective. Economic theories of religious behaviour assume that people acquire religion in the same way that they acquire other objects of their choice. They evaluate its costs and benefits and acts so as to optimise their utility. As in any market, the consumers' freedom is to choose constraints, the producers of religion. It determines the content of religious commodities and the structure, where religion is unregulated and, as a result, a competition among religious firms is pronounced.

The 'Economic Study of Religion' includes some different concepts. These are:

(1) It is a study of the current and historic role of religion in advancing or impeding economic development, social progress, moral development, scientific and technological advances, and so forth.

(2) It is the economic study of religious beliefs, behaviour, and institutions which explain the conversion and commitment that emphasise choice and rationality over irrationality and indoctrination.

(3) It focusses on the religion oriented critiques of economic theory and practice, i.e., religion-oriented critiques of capitalism, socialism, materialism, specific economic practices.

(4) It is a study of religious 'markets'. This economic theory of religious particularities is the alternative to traditional 'secularisation' theory that emphasises the centrality of

innovation, entrepreneurship and competition at the 'religious market place'.

(5) The commitment of this study and the religious groups that influence the well-being of individuals, families, youth, commodities and nations.

(6) It considers the policy implications regarding the state regulation of religion, religious liberty, temple-state relationships, the treatment of minority and deviant faiths, etc.

In contrast to other socio-scientific approaches to this study of religion, the economic approach rests upon the fundamental assumptions of economic analysis, maximising behaviour, stable preferences and market equilibrium. Any study of religious trends states the personal and social determinants of religiosity, the relationship between religious and political or social or economic activities.

Therefore, by these definitions, we can say that in Tarakeswer, every economic activity is governed by the religious activities of the Temple of *Taraknath*. The discussion so far reveals a rich array of ideas and concepts that has shaped this particular field. However, now we have to go to the detailed literature survey. This is our task in the next chapter.

3

Some Earlier Studies

3.1 Introduction

Economists take interest in the question why some countries are rich and why some countries are poor. Differences in labour productivity, inflation, saving and investment rates are the explanations of traditional economics for variations in wealth across the countries. But when these explanations fall short, then the researchers sometimes turn to the non-economic factors like country's legal and social institutions. Another non-economic factor, 'religious factor', can also help explain the variations in the economic growth (Kevin L. Kliesen and Frank A. Schmid, 2004).

Economists avoid different theological questions about the nature of 'God'. But they can illuminate the earthly concern of how people 'buy' and 'sell' the goods and services—material and spiritual—that religious organisations provide (*Business Week Outline*, December, 2004). That's why, a very hiatus, economists have begun to study the relationship between economics and religion. Although some research works interest economic consequences of religiosity, most applied standard economic theory to the study of individual religious activity, the characteristics of religious groups and the impact of regulation and competition on religious markets (*Business Week Outline*, 2004).

In order to comprehend the basic thinking about the economics of religion, it is necessary to segregate between two stands of thinking. Firstly, we consider the literature that is classical and deals with the broader general aspect of the subject. This literature sets the basic framework of the study. However, in the next section, we consider some specific studies, basically those that deal with the socio-economic features of some specific religious sites. It is these latter studies that open-up the main argument of our thesis.

3.2 General Studies

Economics and religion have generally been as separate as chalk and cheese. Adam Smith (1776) delved into religion in 1776 classic '*The Wealth of Nations*'. According to him, one of religion's most important contributions to the economic development process is its value as a moral enforcement mechanism. He also argued that, in a society imbued with these religious mechanisms, some resources will be devoted to determining the veracity of an individual's or firm's business ethics—that economists call the credit or default risk associated with lending to an unknown individual. Moreover, according to him, in societies where there is a widespread belief of 'God', the values of honesty and integrity are more prevalent.

Adam Smith laid the foundation for the economic analysis of religion in a largely ignored chapter of the '*Wealth of Nations*' [(1776) 1965: pp. 740-760]. Here he argued that self-interest motivates clergy, just as it does secular producers; that market forces constrain churches just as they do secular firms and that the benefits of competition; the burden of monopoly, and the hazards of government regulation are as real for religion as for any other sector of the economy.

From eighteenth and nineteenth centuries, a more naturalistic approach was developed Karl Marx (1844), who examines religion from an objective. From the scientific perspective, Marx's analysis and critique of religion is perhaps one of the most famous and most quoted by theists and atheists alike. According to Marx, religion is a phrase of material realities and economic injustice in a given society. So, the problems in religion are the problems of society. It merely is a symptom but not a disease. It is used by oppressors to make people bring poor and exploited. This is the origin of Marx's comment that religion is the 'opium of masses'—a critique of

Hegel's *'Philosophy of Law'*. Therefore, according to Marx, religion is the opium of the people because it is a sigh of oppressed creature, the heart of the heartless world, just as it is the spirit of a spiritless situation (Daniel Pals, *Karl Marx's Interpretation of History*, Bober M.M. and other literatures by Engels F., Peter L. Berger, Jande Varies *et al*).

Marx wrote, 'The religious world is but the reflex of the real world.' He opines that religion has no independent history but is instead the creature of productive forces. In fact, religion is only dependent upon economics, nothing else—so much so that the actual religious doctrines are also irrelevant, which depend upon the social purpose that itself serves not the content of its belief.

Marx's opinion is that religion is meant to create illusory fantasies for the poor, which provide reasons and excuses to keep society functioning just as it is. Economic realities prevent them from finding true happiness in this life, but religion tells this is 'OK' because the true happiness is obtained by them in the next life, i.e., it is treated as opiate-based drugs to the distressed people.

Rebert H. Nelson (2001) is the author of *'Economics of Religion'*. According to him, economics is a system of belief with powerful moral implication. He used the term 'religion' in a broad sense that provides a framework for one's value or some purpose to one's life. He was convinced that people must have some sort of religion, that no one can live entirely free from the framework of meaning. Many economists explain the nature of the world in economic terms, so Nelson refers to economic theology. Such as, the members of the economic profession like 'priests' do the functions of economic programmes. The economic progress has been the leading secular religion of the modern age, especially since the late 19th century and the progressive era (Interview: Robert H. Nelson).

Nelson advocated that the cultural explanations be virtually illegitimate, considered by different economists. When the economists failed to explain an economic development by any other means, then it might be forced to restore to culture. According to him, the economists and social scientists tend to take preference as given. If any belief culture is relating to economic progress, and if anyone wants to do something to stimulate greater progress, then he has to talk about changing the culture, or even religion. But by talking with an economist, the best way to achieve more rapid economic growth would be the change of people's religion, he would puzzled.

According to Nelson, there are two types of economic theologians. Firstly, an economist, who is doing functions as a theologian of the religion of progress by helping to provide an ethical foundation for the society. If the economic progress is the route to rescue, these priests will be the experts on how to achieve that progress. Due to this knowledge, the society looks to and they logically become the leading priesthood of the age. Secondly, an economic theologian is to study economics from a theological perspective. Nelson strives to be something of an economic theologian of this type.

Among the Indian scholars, Vidhatri (1979) was the first who made an attempt to study the places of Hindu pilgrimage. He agrees with the view that there was an important role of pilgrimage in the field of Indian civilisation. According to him, pilgrims are the *'consumers of the sacred'*. He discussed about the casual treatment of the pilgrims. Various anthropologists and sociologists have considered the demographic, socio-cultural, economic relations and other characteristics of the sacred centres for the relevance of the pilgrimage of that place (Vidhatri, LP, Jha, M. and Saraswati, 1979).

By Arnold Toynbee (1954) in *'A Study of History'*, it is pointed out that the Indian civilisation shows a definite tendency towards pre-dominantly religious outlook. Redfield (1955) advocated that the study of the traditional centres could provide valuable information about the complexity of Indian civilisation and social organisation of tradition. According to him, the concepts of different traditions have paved the way for studying the temples and places of pilgrimage (Chopra P. N. 1982).

Another interesting study is by Montalvo and Reynal-Querol (2002). They have developed a religious polarisation index. They found that per capita income and investment, human capital of a nation is inversely related with this measure of religious polarisation. However, the population growth is positively related with it.

Eminent economist, Milton Friedman (2004), once said that free market and American-style religious pluralism have gone hand-in-hand, stimulating both economic growth and religion. Similarly, by Carmel U. Chiswick, American religious practices have adopted to economic conditions. In America, time is more expensive, so they have come to spend less time—though often more money—on religion. Chiswick said that 'when something gets expensive, you try to fig. out ways of satisfying the same wants more cost effectively' (*Business Week Outline*, December 6, 2004).

In *Imagining Religion*, Jouathan Z. Smith (1982) writes that 'while there is a staggering amount of data, phenomena of human experiences and expressions that might be characterised in one culture or another, yet one criterion or another, as religion'—that is, there is no data for religion. Therefore, according to him, religion does not really exist; rather there is culture (Jouathan Z. Smith).

The best definition of religion is seen in '*The Encyclopaedia of Philosophy*'. It schedules traits of religious rather then declaring religion to be one thing or another, arguing that the more markers present in a belief system.

In the present century, most of the systematic studies on religious culture, pilgrim centres and their pilgrimage activities were initiated, particularly, by the anthropologists, sociologists, and historians.

According to Alexis de Tocqueville (1951), early in the nineteenth century, in America, it is said that religion did not impart a taste for freedom and it facilitated the use of free institutions. He also states that a religious country lessened its dependence on the public sector, which not only left a large amount of resources for the private sector but also enhanced the country's moral fiber (Kevin L. Kliesen and Frank A. Schmid, 2004).

German sociologist, Max Weber (1958), said that capitalism developed in Western Europe and America much before any other parts of the world. In the orient world of India, China could not have happened middle East-Asia, due to a 'particular ethos was lacking'. The ethos that set the protestants apart from all other religions and which facilitated economic growth, which was an intense commitment to work, dependability diligence, self-denial, austerity, thrift, punctuality, fulfillment of promises and fidelity to group interests. He also opined that the Protestants were in much better position than others (Kevin L. Kliesen and Frank A. Schmid, 2004).

According to the secularisation hypothesis supported by economists, Edward Glaeser and Bruce Sacerdote (2002), as the country's inhabitants become richer and more educated, their faith in religion and religious inhabitants waves and they attend less regularly. They advocated that increased education will lead to a reduction in the extent of religious beliefs. Therefore, there is strife with the traditional religious beliefs. But the economist, Laurence R. Iannaccone (1998) does not agree with this view. According to him, the church attendance rise with education that suggests that rich western countries should have higher rates of church attendance. Moreover, he said that the academies ignored religion in part out of a belief that would fade under the onslaught of secularisation (Kevin L. Kliesen and Frank A. Schmid, 2004).

Most of the economists of religion think that a *laissez-faire* approach to religion works is the best. Laurence R. Iannaccone argues that United States was the world's first free market for religion. He harks back to Adam Smith, who advocated that competition among faiths would make religion "free from every mixture of absurdity imposture, or fanaticism". It may be hard to find 'God' in supply-and-demand curves, but that is not stopping economists from bringing their own special insights to religion (By Joseph Weber and Peter Coy).

Some scholars believed caste is a distinctive feature of the Hindu religion [*Religious and Communities of India*—PN. Chopra (1982)]. Moreover, division of labour and the functional differentiation has been regarded as a very important feature of the caste system and, of course, guaranteed economic interdependence of the various castes (Damle YB). According to Mahatma Gandhi, religion covers the whole gamut of life in this country, India.

Douglass North (2005), focussed on cultural factors. He takes into account religion as a central element of almost all cultures. Economists try to fit culture and religious factors into some kind of formal model with some mathematics or regression analysis or other statistics (Interview: Robert H. Nelson).

Religion is always favourite concern of sociologists and social anthropologists. But economists refuse to touch religion, since it is regarded as *prima facie* arational if not actually irrational. According to the sociologist, Weber, religion is involved with the problem of ultimate meaning with work-a-day life [Damle YB (1982)].

Comte (1988), exhibits the stages of development from the theological to the scientific stage. The former stage is regarded as primitive and the latter being most advanced stage of human development. With the development of rationality and scientific spirit, religion would retreat into the background, even to the point of extinction (*Positivism*-Comte).

3.3 Some Socio-economic Studies

The eminent economist, Stein (1960), discussed the problem of economic networks of Tirumala Tirupati temple. In his analysis, he described, how a sacred institution is catering to the secular function of the outside of society. The study by him is concerned with the economic aspects of the growth of the Tirupati temple to the middle of sixteenth century. It treats with the resources conferred upon the temple by the devotees and with the secular or business organisation of the temple. The analysis by Stein of the Tirupati temple and other temples during medieval period advocated that the nature, origins and utilisation of land and money as religious endowments to the temple redirect it as an important economic regional centre. From the study, Stein concludes that temples served as centres for the redistribution of resources, particularly state resources, has emerged from the study of the Tirupati temple's irrigation programme and the similar activities in other South Indian temples during the medieval period (Stein, Brunton, 1960).

Another study is by Freeman (1975), on the directions of religious change in Kapileswar, a temple village and suburb of Bhubaneswar, the capital of the state of Orissa in Eastern India. In this study, he examines the impact of scarcity, rapid socio-economic changes and urbanisation on this traditional Hindu pilgrimage centre. According to him, rapid urbanisation and modernisation of adjacent areas of pilgrim centre led to simplifying and abandoning the temple services. This is not the disintegration of religion or the rise of secularisation; rather the attention of religion fluctuated from temple deity to expression of popular religion like Trinath Mela, annual fire walking and physical ordeal ceremony, festival of *Durga Puja*, etc., in Bhubaneswar. He asserts that such popular performances were more flexible and barriers of caste were loosened and they also provide various new opportunities for the hard-pressed ritual associates (James M. Freeman, 1975). However, Freeman (1975), made no attempt to quantify the religious attractiveness of the site.

The sociologist, Dr P Chakraborty (1984), discusses on the social structure of Tarakeswar, a place of Hindu pilgrimage in West Bengal. He traced the social structure of sacred complex, activities of social organisation of priests, social and economic characteristics of pilgrims, pilgrimage activities of Tarakeswar, trend of change in pilgrims' characteristics, social composition and behavioural pattern of a section of pilgrims, economic functions of different ritual associates, etc. From his analysis, we come to know about the dimensions of the pilgrimage activities and relations, as well as changes at Tarakeswer.

Guido Heineck (2001), examined the interrelationship between religious behaviour of an individual and various socio-economic and demographic factors.. According to him, religious attainment is directly related to the different socio-economic variables like age and denominational affiliations, but it can't be explained by other independent variables. The similar studies are done by Das and Datta (2001 and 2003), on Hindu pilgrimage in India.

Rachel M McCleary and Barro (2003), speculated that the high levels of religious belief can positively stimulate economic growth. They perhaps said that the religious faith may sustain aspects of individual behaviour that enhance productivity, which perhaps includes honesty and openness to strangers. According to them, the religious beliefs influence individual traits that enhance economic performance. In their study, they opine that the beliefs are, in turn, the principal output of the religion sector, and church attendance measures the inputs to this sector. They showed, for given beliefs, more church attendance signifies more resources used up by the religion sector (Rachel M McCleary and Robert J Barro, April, 2003).

In a paper, they also show with evidence the negative relation between the church attendance and economic growth. According to them, increased church attendance could reduce the economic growth, since more resource flowing to the religious sector. But to Weber (1958), there is a positive relation between religious activities and economic growth. They believed by spurring individual behaviour and action that are thought to encourage productivity, raises the economic growth. So, the net effect of religious activity on economic growth is uncertain. For that reason, Barro and McCleary (2003) both found that economic preference was largely unrelated to the dominant religious theology of the nation.

Some studies on the economics of rural pilgrimage were presented by Baby (2003) in his project conducted by Kerala Reserch Programme on Local Level Development (KRPLLD) at Erumely gram panchayat, Kerala. In her project, she shows how Sabari pilgrimage generates socio-cultural, economic and environmental effects throughout Kerala. According to her, there is a paradigm shift in the occupational pattern of the households in the pilgrim seasons. She also opines that the Sabari pilgrimage produces cost of both quantifiable (such as increased cost of living) and non-quantifiable (such as the effect of increased congestion, probable increase in crime, pollution, diseases and threats to traditional values) effect on the way of life of households in the rural areas (Dr Baby, April 2003).

The opinion of many economists is that the religious economics studies how religions affect economic growth. Prof Timur Kuran's (2004), argument is that the development of Muslim countries has been hindered historically by certain rules of the sacred religious book, *Koran*, very powerful force in contemporary society (*Business Week Outline*, 2004).

More recently, the Muslim world has accepted the legal conventions of corporate life, with modernisers such as Turkey and Malaysia in the lead. But Kuran, in his new book, *Islam and Mammon: The Economic Predicaments of Islamism*, says the long-delayed modernisation 'started from a low base, and it's been trailing ever since.'

Alberini and Longo (2006), presented their paper on the travel cost method with contingent behaviour questions to estimate domestic visitors' use values of cultural heritage sites in Armenia. In this paper, they combine the actual trip with the stated trip under hypothetical programmes by fitting a panel data model that would enhance the conservation of four monuments and improve the cultural experience, quality of infrastructure, service of the site, etc. Their investigation also shows the significant use value which associated with the study and conservation of the cultural heritage sites, improve the cultural experience as well as tourist services that encourage the higher visitation rates by making it easier for the respondents to reach and spend time at this cultural site (Alberini and Longo, 2006).

A paper by David B. Audretsch, Werner Boente and Jagannadha Pawan Tamvada (2007), reveals the impact of religion on the economic decision-making process of individuals. The study examines the influence of religion on the decision of people to become an entrepreneur. This paper explores that religion shapes the entrepreneurial decision based on a large-scale data set of nearly ninety thousand workers in India. In particular, some religions, such as Islam and Christianity, are found to be conducive to entrepreneurship, while others, such as Hinduism, restrain entrepreneurship. This paper also links the decision of people in India to start a business to their religion as well as their caste status. Thus, caste system is found to influence the propensity to become an entrepreneur. Individuals belonging to a backward caste exhibit a lower propensity to become an entrepreneur. Thus, on the basis of the empirical evidence, the study suggests that both religion and the tradition of the caste system influence entrepreneurship, suggesting a link between religion and economic behaviour.

An effective measurement of cultural value was done by Choi, Papandrea and Bennett (2007). According to them, non-market valuation method such as Contingent Valuation Technique and Choice Modelling are not suitable to encapsulate the full value of cultural goods due to the multidimensional nature of cultural value. They offer some theoretical variables known as latent variables that are likely to help explain the multidimensional nature of these cultural values. In their article, they develop a Cultural Worldwide Scale to measure the people's general attitude and behaviour such as primitive belief and perception in the perceived cultural value, represented by the latent variables. By developing Cultural Worldwide Scale, they explained how people's attitudes influence their determination of cultural values by using factor and cluster analysis. In this study, they use four factors such as cultural linkage, recognition of cultural values, cultural loss and preservation of tradition and customs to comprise the Cultural Worldwide Scale on the basis of two separate economic valuation studies of Old Parliament House and National Museum of Australia in Canberra (Andy S. Choi, Papandrea F. and Bennett J., October, 2007).

From a Bengali book, titled '*Glimpses on the History of Tarakeswar and Foundation of Tarakeswar Temple*', written by N Senapati (2002), we may perceive the information about the legend *Taraknath*, date and early history of origin of temple of *Taraknath* at Tarakeswar. This book also displays the information about the *Mohantas*, the history of the establishment of the temple, and the hinterland of *Tarakeswar*, impact of the temple in modern epoch, impact of the river Damodar, etc.

In this chapter, we have discussed in detail the prevailing mode of thinking in the mainstream literature on the role of religious culture and its impact on the mainstream economic activities. It is clear that almost all the thinkers opine the crucial role that religion plays in determining the socio-economic fabric of the society that man has erected. However, we require a rigorous quantitative documentation of these phenomena at a micro-level from an economist's viewpoint. Such analysis would help us juxtapose the broader macro-fabric that all the thinkers visualise. Very few studies in this regard are available at hand. These bring out the importance of the present study and its role in a broader fabric. In the next chapter, we set out the path by discussing about the data structure and methodology used in the study.

Note

1. This argument may fail for Hindu religion. Hindu religion has two spheres – a private sphere and a public sphere. Lots of religious activities might be concentrated in the private sphere without affecting the public sphere.

4

Data Used in the Study

4.1 Introduction

In this research study, we have unveiled a new area of non-traditional economic discussion that there is a relation between Religious Culture and Economic Culture. In this study, we discuss how the Economic Culture is derived by the Temple Culture at Tarakeswar. The confirmation or refutation of the economic interpretation on the new field, that is Religious Culture, specifically Temple Culture, on the basis of statistical investigation, which began with the collection of data. In order to examine this amalgamation between Temple Culture and the Social-economic Culture, we analyse various types of data by employing different types of statistical techniques which are used in the study.

4.2 Data Used

These data are collected from field investigation. During the field investigation, we used the following methods like observation, interview, genealogy, household enumeration and information from correspondents. The survey was made in the year 2007-2008, through personal questionnaire method by using structured and open-ended questionnaire schedule at different places like railway station, bus stand, different rest houses, different shops, etc. at Tarakeswar.

(a) Data Collection from Pilgrims

The primary data on the various socio-economic features of these pilgrims and their interaction with the local hospitality providers at this sacred centre are collected by interviewing 733 pilgrims who arrived at Tarakeswar to fulfill their religious requirements.

(b) Data Collection from Local Hospitality Providers

In this study, we also analyse these types of primary data which are collected from the sacred and secular local hospitality providers like private priests, pilgrim guides, various shopkeepers, restaurant and hotel owners, etc. in the year 2007-2008 at Tarakeswar Municipality area and its surrounding areas of Tarakeswar in West Bengal. A random sample technique was used for collection of data from both male and female respondents, belonging to various income and occupational groups with different educational levels. The information would be collected from 56 samples of sacred service providing group, which is constructed by merging private priest and pilgrim guide and 115 samples of secular hospitality providing group of beneficiaries by interview and also by systematic observations of these beneficiaries.

In order to evaluate the economic effect of temple culture at this sacred centre, Tarakeswar, we analyse the collected data by utilising various types of statistical techniques in the study. These techniques are discussed in the methodology section given below.

Note

1. (a) The detailed discussion on the primary data collection from pilgrims and local hospitality providers is given in chapters 5 and 6, respectively.

   (b) Questionnaire Schedules of both pilgrims and local hospitality providers are given in Appendix I and II.

5

Workers, Consumers and Providers in the 'Sacred' Market

5.1 Introduction

Religious activities are the activities of individual human beings. Though these activities have important social and economic consequences, they are guided by individual activity. In the economics of religion, it is argued that a man behave rationally even while undertaking the religious activity, except in some very special circumstances. In this study, we wish to consider the myriad of human decisions that shape religious activities. We will also consider the web of relationship that develops between man and man while delving into these activities. We take into account both the demand and supply side. The pilgrims, their attitudes and behaviours constitute the demand side of religious activity. On the other hand, there are a number of people, who are associated with providing these activities. Both of them are assumed to behave rationally, i.e., they evaluate its costs and benefits and acts so as to optimise their utility.

The economic study of religion is a study of the modern and historic role of religion in advancing or impeding economic development, social progress, moral prosperity, scientific and technological advances and so forth. The commitment of this study and the religious groups both influence the well-being of individuals, families, youth, commodities and the nation.

From ancient to recent times, the religious culture acts as amender of human being to the whole society. In the different times in the past, separate individuals and community were initiated to change the society and economy on the basis of religious grounds. For example, Mahaprabhu Sri Chaitanya, Gautam Buddha, Jesus Christ, Hajrat Mohammad, etc., are those high souled persons from different religions who amended the human's society, whose impact falls in the field of the country and also in their economy.

The importance of any religious place not only depends upon the religious establishment, but also relies on the patron of that religion. From the pre-historic stage to the modern civilisation, the socio-economic development of any religious centre is based on the religious heredity as well as the religious supremacy among the people of that place. We see that religion plays a dominant role in humans' life, since time the society was formed. From historical evidence, the society's activities were defined by the religious activities – 'a faith from pre-civilisation' and in the modern society it still exists yet other avenues are generated. We know there were immense contributions of various religious establishments like temple, church, monastery, mosque, etc. in the Indian civilisation as well as in European civilisation for the socio-economic upliftment of the society.

In India, there are many sacred centres associated with different religious faiths. Amongst them, a large number are associated with the Hindu religion. Temple is the sign of deity for Hindus. From the ancient times, the temple was the centre of economic, political and social activities and even it was found to be the centre of power (in the Southern Chola Empire).

On the other hand, interests of people for religion also have profuse contribution for socio-economic development of any sacred place. Like the traditional economic analysis, the study of economics of religion is the study of religious markets from where people can fulfill their rational choice for religious particularities. That is, both the consumers (pilgrims) and the suppliers can optimise their ritual utility from religious goods. Therefore, an important part is to study the rational calculations that go behind the consumers of those particular goods, i.e., pilgrims and also behind the suppliers, i.e., sacred and secular hospitality providers.

Tarakeswar is a famous place of Hindu pilgrimage of West Bengal, mainly due to the temple of 'Lord Shiva'. A large number of people come to this place from near and far to fulfill their religious requirements. In this sacred centre, people do network of social and economical association in a number of diverse ways in spite of their various social hierarchies and nature of occupations. Again, the increased flow of pilgrims in a large number to this sacred centre has produced a hopeful impact upon certain spheres of social and economic life of Tarakeswar. So, the importance and development of this pilgrim town, Tarakeswar, is not only almost for the religious endowment to 'Lord Shiva' but also depends upon the behaviour of both consumers and suppliers of the particular goods (i.e., religious goods).

In this chapter, we first introduce the micro-level analysis of the Temple Culture. Here, we make a micro-level discussion on the pilgrims, who are the consumers of this particular culture and also on the sacred and secular (non-sacred) local hospitality providers, who supply this culture. The present work does attempt to explore the socio-economic profile of the pilgrims, on the one hand, and, on the other hand, we also illuminate the socio-economic dependency of the sacred groups, i.e., temple employees like priests, pilgrim guides, etc. and also the secular group like manager, accountant, treasurer, guards, sweepers, maid servants, etc., under Temple Estate Authority and rest house owners, shopkeepers, restaurant owners, florists, potters, etc., under the local hospitality group. The concerned study also deals with the examinations that whether people under different occupational groups at this sacred town can earn their livelihood by offering different religious and non-religious services to the pilgrims or not. Along with the study, we also examine the degree of devotion for this particular culture by the pilgrims. Therefore, this study conveys the message that in non-traditional field of economics, Religious Culture is one of the important non-economic factors, which is responsible for the socio-economic development of any sacred centre.

5.2 Pilgrims (Socio-economic and Cultural Profile)

India has numerous sacred places with various religious faiths among which a large number are associated with Hinduism. Any discussion about a pilgrimage centre never become complete without considering its pilgrim component, which is one of the vital factors for development of that place, is taken into account. The frequent flows of pilgrims to these sacred places enunciate the important role that these religious centres play in our society. In Eastern India, Tarakeswar is one of the famous sacred places of Hindu pilgrimage, since more than a centaury and a half. It enticed many devotees to this sacred place from far and near. The considerable importance and development are mainly due to the pilgrimage activity at Tarakeswar. So, we can say that without *'Baba Taraknath',* the town of Tarakeswar has nearly nothing.

In the present study, we examine the social, economic and cultural behaviour of pilgrims at Tarakeswar. It is very important, since the purpose of pilgrimage varies in relation to the social background of any sacred place. It is revealed that the prosperity of the town depends immensely upon the visit of the pilgrims and any unfavorable things occur in the visits towards Tarakeswar, causing inconvenience to the economic condition of this pilgrimage town, Tarakeswar.

As a place of Hindu pilgrimage, Tarakeswar has now reached the phenomenal height; millions of devotees come to this sacred place from diverse areas for a long time. According to Vidyarthi, pilgrims are those who are the 'consumers of sacred'. The people, who retain its ritual customs to a great extent and also maintain the economic stability and make the centre popular, are called the pilgrims. Simply, those people, who come to the holy place to fulfill their religious requirements, are called pilgrims. That is, the pilgrims act as value-receptors.

There are many religious festivals that are celebrated at Tarakeswar. Out of them, three important festivals are *'Sivaratri'*, *'Chaitra Sankranti'* and *'Sravani Purnima'* on which a large number of pilgrims congregate here to fulfill their religious requirements. Besides these, the assemblage of pilgrims rises remarkably on every Sunday, Monday and usual holidays throughout the year. Therefore, the divine grace or sublimity of *'Baba Taraknath'* attracts many devotees from diverse areas to Tarakeswar for a long time.

Pilgrims (commonly referred to as *'yatris'*) at this sacred place are differentiated into three categories. These are *'sada yatris'*, *'jal yatris'* and *'dharna yatris'*. We have already discussed about them in the previous chapter. The pilgrims who usually come to Tarakeswar by train, bus or other transports are called *'sada yatris'*. That is, the regular pilgrims are regarded as *'sada yatris'*. They visit this sacred place without wearing any special dresses. The next one is *'jal yatris'*, who come to Tarakeswar, carrying the sacred water of *'Ganga'* in the small vessels slung at the two ends of yoke pole on their neck. They pour a few drops of sacred water on the deity, known as *'Baba Loknath'* on the way to Tarakeswar. The *'jal yatris'* make their journey all the way on bare foot, wearing red or ochre coloured shirts and vests, except women. These pilgrims generally come to Tarakeswar in the month of *'Sravan'* (July-August). That's why, these are called *'Sravani yatris'*. Some *'jal yatris'* also visit this place on the occasion of *'Chaitra Sankranti'* in the month of *'Chaitra'* (i.e., March-April).

According to the nature of contact with the priests at Tarakeswar, the pilgrims are classified into three categories. These are, *'Natun yatris'*, *'Alapi yatris'* and *'Dalal yatris'*. Those pilgrims are called *'Natun yatris'*, who reach their priest through their own effort or on the other hand, the priests secure them personally also with their own efforts. The new and unknown pilgrims are generally named as *'Nutan yatris'*. Besides these, some pilgrims are collected by the pilgrim guides and are assisted by the priest in order to fulfill their religious requirements. These pilgrims are called *'Dalal yatris'*. The relationship of pilgrims with the priests as well as pilgrim guides is transitory and contractual in nature. It implies that on the prior condition of the payment of a fixed sum, the priests offer some sort of informal services to these pilgrims to fulfill their ritual needs. Again, some pilgrims are called *'Alapi yatris'*, who come out from previous familiarity with the priests. From the traditional clientele association with the priests, these pilgrims come to Tarakeswar by their personal visit or by postal correspondence.

Like the nature of contact with the priest, the pilgrims are also categorised on the basis of the purpose of visit. From the divergence of purpose of visit of the sacred place, the pilgrims are differentiated into various types, namely, *'dharna yatris'*, *'upanayan yatris'*, etc. People quite often visit this sacred place not only for devotion but also to obtain the deity's favour for the fulfillment of their materialistic gains. Pilgrims usually come to Tarakeswar to fulfill their three motives, i.e., spiritual motives, material motives and recreational motives. Under spiritual motives, people come to this religious place for *'darshan'* (auspicious view of the deity), *'punya'* (religious merit), *'pap-skhalan'* (redemption of sins) and *'mukti'* (salvation). The material motives include such desires, which implicate the therapeutic, socio-cultural and economic aspects. The therapeutic motives are associated with the problems of health like curing the diseases, revive health and so on. The socio-cultural motives provide such requirements which are related with the social, rites, ritual duties, etc. of the pilgrims like *'upanayana'* (investiture with sacred thread), *'annaprason'* (first sacred rice taking of child), *'mundan'* (tonsure), etc. On the other hand, the economic motives consider the progress in business, promotion of services, getting employment, termination of property concerned disputes and so on. On the basis of faith in *'Baba Taraknath'* by the people to solve the material problems spread out the popularity of the deity of Tarakeswar.

Like the fulfillment of spiritual and material needs, people also come to Tarakeswar for recreational purposes. Desire for change in the monotonous daily life, for curiosity about this historical religious place, fun and amusement and for recreation, many people visit Tarakeswar. To these people, the deity or the religious importance of this pilgrim centre, Tarakeswar represents nothing more than a religious tourist spot.

Socio-cultural Profile of Pilgrims

In this section, we discuss about the social, cultural and economic characteristics of the pilgrims, who come to Tarakeswar to fulfill their religious requirements. The discussion is based on the data collected from a sample of 733 pilgrims at different points of time in the year 2007. The field investigation was conducted among the pilgrims by the interview method on the basis of structured and open-ended questionnaire schedules. The survey is spread over the year into three different occasions. In order to get appropriate coverage, we collected data from those periods in which the attendance of pilgrims is (i) maximum, (ii) minimum and (iii) the period in between them. While the data was collected by interview, the information about the pilgrimage activities was also gathered by systematic observations of the pilgrims' behaviour.

Social Characteristics

The deity of *'Baba Taraknath'* attracts many people from diverse areas to Tarakeswar for a long time. The field investigation displays that pilgrims come to this sacred place not only from West Bengal but also from other states like Bihar, Assam, Jharkhand and Odisha. The percentage distribution of pilgrims by the area of origin can be shown by the Table 1:

Table 1: Percentage Distribution of Pilgrims from Different Districts and States

State	*District*	*No. of Pilgrims*	*Percentage No. to Total Sample*
West Bengal	Kolkata	157	21.4
	Howrah	122	16.6
	Hooghly	71	9.7
	Burdwan	66	9.0
	Bankurah	10	1.4
	Birbhum	23	3.1
	Nadia	30	4.1
	Murshidabad	20	2.8
	North 24-Pargana	33	4.5
	South 24-Pargana	48	6.6
	Midnapur	129	17.6
	Purulia	7	1.0
Jharkhand		7	1.0
Bihar		2	0.3
Assam		2	0.3
Odisha		5	0.7
Total		**733**	**100**

Source: Author's survey.

Table 1 shows that overwhelmingly a large portion of sample pilgrims come from different districts of West Bengal. The percentage number of pilgrims to total sample pilgrims is 97.7, those who come from various districts like Howrah, Hooghly, Burdwan, Bankurah, Birbhum, Nadia, Murshidabad, North 24-Pargana, South 24-Pargana, Midnapur, Purulia and Kolkata, the capital city of West Bengal. Among these districts, the maximum percentage of pilgrims would come from the capital city of Kolkata, i.e., 21.4 per cent, to Tarakeswar. Amazingly, the percentage number of visits by the pilgrims from Midnapur district is higher than all other districts. It is 17.6 per cent. Among all the districts of West Bengal, pilgrims' field extends to twelve districts. Nearly 75 per cent of total sample pilgrims of West Bengal come from Kolkata, Howrah, Hooghly, Burdwan and Midnapur, and 23 per cent pilgrims come from rest of the districts. Only two per cent pilgrims to total sample visit Tarakeswar from out of West Bengal, i.e., from other states like Bihar, Jharkhand, Assam and Odisha. In the month of *'Chaitra'*, i.e., during the period of *'Gajan'*, some pilgrims also come from Bangladesh. Therefore, the table represents the popularity of Tarakeswar due to the deity of *'Baba Taraknath'*, spread out all over West Bengal as well as in the Eastern India and also in the areas outside of India.

Religious practices are different among different group of people living in the cities, towns and villages. Pilgrimage is a part of religious activities. So, the pilgrimage activities are also different among the people living in cities, towns and villages. The percentage distribution of pilgrims from cities, towns and villages is shown in Table 2.

Table 2: Percentage Distribution of Pilgrims from Cities, Towns and Villages to Total Sample

Sector of Origin	*No. of Pilgrims*	*Percentage No. of Pilgrims to the Total Sample*
City	220	30
Town	190	25.9
Village	323	44.1
Total	**733**	**100**

Source: Author's survey.

Table 2 shows that a large percentage of pilgrims to the total sample pilgrims comes from villages. It is 44.1 per cent, which is larger than the percentage attendance of pilgrims from cities and towns, respectively. The percentage of pilgrims' attendance from cities and towns is 30 and 25.9, respectively. Therefore, the information exhibits that the deity of *'Baba Taraknath'* at Tarakeswar influences the urban inhabitants more compared to the village inhabitants.

Cultural Behaviour of Pilgrims

According to Bharadwaj (1973), different places of Hindu sacred centres are associated with the specified caste. Even though the pilgrims from all castes like general castes, schedule castes and schedule tribes come to Tarakeswar for their religious requirements.

The examination on caste composition of pilgrims are represented in Table 3:

Table 3: Percentage Distribution of Pilgrims According to the Caste Composition

Caste Group	*No. of Pilgrims*	*Percentage No. of Pilgrims to Total Sample*
General Castes	476	65
Schedule Castes	227	31
Schedule Tribes	29	4
Total	**733**	**100**

Source: Author's survey.

Table 3 exhibits that 65 per cent of the total pilgrims come from certain common castes, which are treated as general castes. Under general castes, most of the pilgrims are Brahmins, Kayasthas, Banias, etc. Besides these, 31 per cent and four per cent pilgrims fall under the category of schedule castes and schedule tribes, respectively. Most of the regular pilgrims and *'Sravani'* pilgrims come from high and middle categories. The *'Gajan'* pilgrims generally belong to the lower category.

Now we examine another cultural feature of the sample pilgrims, i.e., family education structure. This socio-cultural feature, i.e., education, gives a broad outline of social background of the various devotees, which is necessarily cultural and it usually has a role in facilitating their religious journey. The socio-cultural behaviour of the pilgrims is directly associated with education. In our investigation, the educational levels of pilgrims are categorised into four levels. These are illiterate, education level up to secondary, up to higher secondary and graduation level or above. The percentage categorisation of pilgrims according to their level of education are represented in Table 4.

Table 4: Percentage Distribution of Pilgrims According to their Level of Education

Level of Education	*No. of Pilgrims*	*Percentage No. of Pilgrims to the Total Sample*
Illiterate	51	7
Up to Secondary	323	44
Up to Higher Secondary	154	21
Graduation or above	205	28
Total	**733**	**100**

Source: Author's survey.

Table 4 shows that more than 90 per cent (i.e., 93 per cent) pilgrims out of total sample pilgrims are literate. Only seven per cent pilgrims are illiterate. The extent of education among literates varies from one pilgrim to another pilgrim. The investigation displays that 44 per cent pilgrims come from secondary level of education and 21 per cent pilgrims are from higher secondary education level. But the pilgrims from higher education level, i.e., from graduation level and above are more than the percentage number of pilgrims from higher secondary education level. The percentage of pilgrims from graduation level or above is 28. The education up to secondary level of the sample pilgrims is higher than the education level up to higher secondary as well as graduation level and above. It is seen that the regular pilgrims are found more in the higher secondary and above category of education; similarly *'Sravani'* pilgrims are larger in secondary and higher secondary levels of education. The illiterate and lowest education levels are found in the *'Gajan'* pilgrims.

Economic Characteristics of Pilgrims

Under the economic characteristics of pilgrims, we consider two types of features: (i) occupational structure of sample pilgrims, and (ii) per capita monthly income of pilgrims' family. From this discussion, we get the degree of devotion by the pilgrims under different economic patterns.

The socio-economic and cultural scenario at Tarakeswar gives a broad picture about the social and economic background of the different types of devotees from different occupational groups. Pilgrimage activity is a performance of volition of own and the participation, which is guided by their occupational and economic condition.

The occupational pattern of the sample pilgrims are represented in Table 5:

Table 5: Percentage Distribution of Pilgrims According to their Occupational Pattern

Pattern of Occupation	*No. of Pilgrims*	*Percentage No. of Distribution of Pilgrims to the Total Sample*
Agriculture	44	6
Business	191	26
Govt. Services	66	9
Non-government Services	161	22
Marginal	117	16
Others	154	21 (17+4)*
Total	**733**	**100**

*17—Self-employed, 4—Unemployed.

Source: Author's survey.

The occupational structures of the pilgrims are classified into six broad categories. These are agriculture, business, government services, non-sovernment services, menial works and others. The menial workers are those, who are doing as the factory workers, plying paddle rickshaws, taxies, auto-rickshaws, making buildings, working as a daily labourers in agriculture and industry, etc. Excepting these so-called professions, some pilgrims are engaged with another category, named 'Others'. In this category, we consider those people, who are self-employed like hawkers as well as students, house-wives, widows and unemployed persons.

Table 5 exhibits that only six per cent pilgrims of the total sample pilgrims are engaged in the agricultural works and another lower percentage, i.e., nine per cent, people under the total sample are associated with government jobs. Most of the pilgrims are doing business and non-government jobs. The percentages are 26 and 22, respectively. There are also 16 per cent pilgrims pursuing menial works. Besides these, there is another category, named 'Others', in which 21 per cent pilgrims are engaged. Under this category, 17 per cent of pilgrims are self-employed and remaining four per cent are not associated with any types of jobs. The investigation shows that the *'Sravani'* pilgrims come relatively more from those families pursuing agricultural works, business, and menial works. The regular pilgrims are usually more from the families, pursuing government services, business, and non-government services. The *'Gajan'* pilgrims come more from menial working groups and other working groups. Also large number of pilgrims visits this sacred place on *'Chaitra Sankranti'* festival, i.e., in *'Gajan mela'* (fair). This examination on pilgrims' occupational pattern gives a rough sketch about the economic position of the pilgrims.

To know the economic conditions of the pilgrims, we make another investigation on the pilgrims' earning structure. In order to get a clear picture about the financial condition of the pilgrims at Tarakeswar, monthly income has been taken into account. From this monthly income, we determine the per capita monthly income by dividing the individual's family income with their total number of family members. The percentage distribution of pilgrims under different income groups are shown in Table 6:

Table 6: Percentage Distribution of Pilgrims under Different Income Groups

Per Capita Income	*No. of Pilgrims*	*Percentage No. of Pilgrims to the Total Sample*
Below – 500	68	9.3
501 – 700	91	12.4
701 – 900	279	38
901 – 1,000	78	10.7
1001 – Above	217	29.6
Total	**733**	**100**

Source: Author's survey.

The per capita monthly incomes of the pilgrims' families are classified into five categories. These are: Rs 500 and less, Rs 501-700, Rs 701-900, Rs 901-1000 and Rs 1001 and above. Table 6 indicates better economic condition of the pilgrims, since from the data, approximately 30 per cent pilgrims of total sample pilgrims lie in the economic group Rs 1001 and above. Maximum number of pilgrims, i.e., 38 per cent pilgrims to the total sample, earns income between Rs 701 and Rs 900. A small percentage (i.e., 9.3 per cent) of total sample earns the lower income of Rs 500 and below. Besides these, other low income groups of Rs 501-700 and Rs 901-1000 include 12.4 per cent and 10.7 per cent pilgrims to the total sample, respectively. It implies that more than 78 per cent pilgrims come from higher financial condition. Mainly the regular pilgrims come from better economic conditions, but the *'Sravani'* and the *'Gajan'* pilgrims come from medium and lower income groups to Tarakeswar. From this analysis, we can say that the deity of *'Baba Taraknath'* attracts many pilgrims from different income groups to Tarakeswar, majority of whom fall in the medium income groups.

On the basis of the above data, we also construct the bi-variate data on the different features of pilgrims. Firstly, we consider the percentage distribution of pilgrims' visit under different per capita income groups from different areas, as given in Table 7.

Table 7: Percentage Distribution of Pilgrims under Different Income Groups according to their Sector of Origin

Sector of Origin	*Below–500*	*501-700*	*701 - 900*	*901-1000*	*1001-above*
City	4.6	5.75	28.74	16.09	44.83
Town	8	14.67	52	10.67	14.67
Village	13.28	15.62	35.94	7.03	28.13

Source: Author's survey.

This table indicates that very small percentage, i.e., 4.6 per cent, of pilgrims with lower income come from cities. But maximum percentage, i.e., 44.83 per cent, of pilgrims under higher income groups come from cities. On the other hand, maximum percentage, i.e., 13.28 per cent, of pilgrims under lower income groups come from villages. The maximum percentages of pilgrims under middle income group come from towns and villages.

Another bi-variate data on literacy structure of pilgrims under different income groups are shown in Table 8.

Table 8: Percentage Distribution of Pilgrims with Different Income Groups according to their Education Level

Education / Income	*Below-500*	*501-700*	*701-900*	*901-1000*	*1001-above*
Illiterate	45	35	15	5	0
Upto Secondary education level	9.3	15.5	52.71	7.75	14.73
Upto Higher Secondary education level	5.08	5.08	45.76	25.42	18.64
Graduation and above	3.66	7.32	14.63	6.1	68.29

Source: Author's survey.

Table shows that the greater percentage of pilgrims, i.e., 45 per cent and 35 per cent, under the lower income groups are illiterate, whereas the greater percentage of pilgrims, i.e., 68.29 per cent, with higher education, graduation or above, come from high income groups. But the maximum percentage, 52.71 per cent and 45.76 per cent, of pilgrims, with secondary and higher secondary level of education, respectively, come from middle income group.

In the same way also constructed another bi-variate data percentage number of pilgrims under different income groups according their various occupational structures, as shown in Table 9.

Table 9: Percentage Distribution of Pilgrims under Different Income Groups according to their Occupational Structure

Occupation/Income	*Below-500*	*501-700*	*701-900*	*901-1000*	*1001-above*
Agriculture	16.67	22.22	38.89	5.55	16.67
Business	6.67	5.33	41.33	9.33	37.33
Govt. Service	0	0	26.92	46.15	26.92
Non-govt. Service	3.08	12.31	53.85	7.69	23.08
Menial Works	23.91	32.61	21.74	8.7	13.04
Other Works	10	8.33	33.33	3.33	45

Source: Author's survey.

Table shows that maximum percentage of pilgrims under different occupational groups come from middle income group, i.e., Rs 701 to Rs 900. Under lower income groups, more pilgrims come from agriculture, non-government services and menial works. On the contrary, under high income groups, pilgrims come from government services, business and other works.

In this way, we can say that the socio-economic and cultural characteristics of pilgrims visit Tarakeswar to fulfill their religious requirements. Our investigation on the social, economic and cultural behaviour of pilgrims represents an interaction between these factors with the religious factors.

5.3 Temple Employees (A Socio-economic Profile)

At every Hindu pilgrimage centre in India, the ritual and non-ritual functions associated with the temple always play an important role in the society as well as in the economy of that place. Although it comprises various categories of people depending upon the temple by doing different ritual and non-ritual functions, but in this chapter we focus on the activities of ritual employees or religious agents only.

By the ritual employees, we mean those people who are directly dependent on the temple by providing various ritual and non-ritual functions. The different categories of ritual employees can be represented by the Fig. 1.

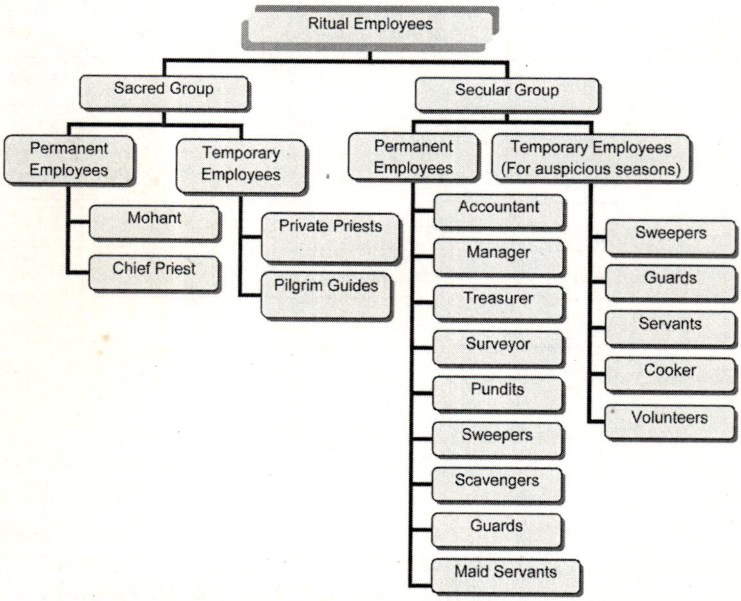

Fig. 1: Different Categories of Ritual Employees.

This Fig. represents that the temple employees can be classified into two categories: (1) Sacred Group, and (2) Secular Group. Under the sacred category, the people do various ritual roles and functions to facilitate devotees in order to fulfill their religious requirements at Tarakeswar and, on the contrary under secular group, people do certain non-ritual activities to patronise the religious activities at Tarakeswar.

The sacred group is also categorised into two groups: (a) Permanent employees, who are appointed by the Temple Estate Authority permanently, and (b) Temporary employees, who provide the different ritual services willingly, i.e., for their self-intension and they are not appointed by the Temple Estate Authority. At Tarakeswar, under sacred group, the permanent employees are *Mohanta*, head of the monastery of *'Baba Taraknath'* and Chief Priest. We have already discussed about them in the earlier chapter..

The head of the monastery as well as the chairman of Temple Estate Authority is *'Mohanta Moharaj'*, who administers the rules and regulations and also controls the activities of Temple Estate Authority at Tarakeswar. As the chief of the Estate Authority and the temple of *'Baba Taraknath'*, he gets Rs 2,000 per month as honorarium from the government. Along with it, he also gets free boarding and lodging from the Temple Estate Authority. In order to manage the Estate Authority's activities conveniently, he appoints various people from time to time. Besides these, on the occasion of *'Guru Purnima'*, many Bengalese and non-Bengalese disciples congregate here at Tarakeswar to pay *'pranamies'* to the *mohanta* for his spiritual guidance. But most of his earnings are spent for philanthropic purposes.

Another permanent employee under sacred group is Chief Priest. He is appointed by the Estate Authority and also approved by the head of the monastery, i.e., *Mohanta*. As a permanent employee, he gets a fixed monthly salary from the Temple Estate Authority. Along with it, he also receives some amount of rice and wheat for his consumption free of cost. The daily ritual of phallic image of *'Lord Siva'* as wells as other gods like *Kali, Laxmi-Narayan, Bara Thakur* (Saturn), *Durga,* etc. is the duty of the Chief Priest. Along with this, he delivers the scriptural and mythological stories on different religious occasions. Sometimes, he is paid by many disciples around Tarakeswar and also Kolkata for imparting spiritual knowledge and officiating in their household ritual ceremonies. From his more than hundred disciples, he receives a regular income in the form of gifts.

Now, we consider the temporary employees under sacred group. It is divided into two categories. These are (i) Private priests, and (ii) Pilgrim guides. Presently, there are 109 private priests, who are engaged with volition at this sacred centre, Tarakeswar. Among them, approximately 86 priests are actively engaged with the priesthood and rests occasionally provide their services for the ritual activities. At most of the Hindu sacred places, more or less homogeneous pattern of socio-cultural and professional levels are maintained by this sacred group.

Socio-cultural Profile

From the commencement of the present century, a substantial number of *'purohits'* (priests) arrived at this place with different social-economic backgrounds. Most of them are originated from Rarhi Brahmin, Acharya Brahmin and Barendra Brahmin of different sections of Bengali Brahmin. They come from different lineages like Ganguli, Chatterjee, Chakraborti, etc. Among them, the Ganguli Brahmins claim themselves as *'Adi-Purohits'* (original priests) and feel proud of their heritage.

Priestcraft at this sacred centre, Tarakeswar, is not impounded exclusively to closed hereditary groups. Priests come to this pilgrimage centre from various neighbouring districts like Burdwan, Bankurah, Howrah, etc. and a few came from Bangladesh before six to seven generations. Besides these, some priests are living in adjoining blocks of Tarakeswar like Haripal, Champadanga, etc.

The pilgrimage centre of Tarakeswar attracts many people into the profession of priestcraft due to expansion of temple rituals, increase in the number of devotees, development in the infrastructural systems like communication (roads and railway transport systems). The experiences of priests in this profession are examined by the field investigation on 64 sample priests at Tarakeswar. The maturity in the occupation of priestcraft is analysed by considering a separate index, named Experience Index. By the Experience Index, we mean,

Experience Index =

$$\frac{\text{(Observed value of working years} - \text{Minimum value of working years)}}{\text{(Maximum value of working years} - \text{Minimum value of working years)}} \times 100$$

The field investigation shows the maximum working years of the priest in this particular profession in 58 years and the minimum working years are 17, i.e., the working experience of sample priests varies from 17 to 58 years. Percentage distribution of priests to the total sample priests according to their experience can be represented by Table 10.

Table 10: Percentage Distribution of the Sample Priests according to their Experience Index at Tarakeswar

Experience Index Percentage	*No. of Priests*	*Percentage of Priests to the Total Sample Priests*
Below – 10	4	7.81
10 – 20	7	12.5
20 – 30	10	17.19
30 – 40	8	14.06
40-50	9	15.62
50-60	5	9.37
60-70	4	7.81
70-80	5	9.37
80-100	4	6.25
Total	**56**	**100**

Source: Author's survey.

The Experience Index (below-10) per cent to (10-30) per cent implies lower and (30-40) per cent to (50-60) per cent implies average experience and the range (60-70) per cent to (80-100) per cent implies greater experience of priest in this profession. Table 10 indicates that 39.05 per cent priests to the total sample priests have average experience and rest of them, 23.43 per cent, have greater experience and 37.5 per cent have lower experience. This table illuminates that minimum experience, i.e., less than 10 per cent experience in this priestcraft profession (below-10) per cent is acquired by 7.8 per cent priests. The maximum number of priests, i.e. 17.19 per cent, have 20 to 30 per cent experience and 50 to 70 per cent experience in this occupation is attained by 17.18 per cent priests to the total sample. The maximum experience, i.e., 80 to 100 per cent, is earned by 6.25 per cent priests at this pilgrimage centre, Tarakeswar. Therefore, it implies that many people at Tarakeswar maintain their livelihood from this priestly profession for a long time.

The literacy levels of the priests at Tarakeswar are higher than the priests at other religious centres. We classify the levels of education of priests into three categories. These are: the number of priests who have passed (i) the secondary level (Madhyamik including education in Sanskrit Toll), (ii) the higher secondary level, and (iii) graduation level and above. The percentage distribution of priests according to their literacy level are shown in Table 11.

Table 11: Percentage Distribution of Sample Priests according to their Education Level

Level of Education	*No. of Priest*	*Percentage No. to Total Sample*
Upto Secondary level	25	43.75
Upto Higher Secondary level	13	23.44
Graduation and above	18	32.81
Total	**56**	**100**

Source: Author's survey.

This table represents that more than 50 per cent (i.e., 56.25 per cent) priests have passed higher secondary levels and 43.75 per cent priests have gone upto secondary level of education. Some of them of latter category have also studied in Sanskrit Toll at Tarakeswar. Among the sample priests, 32.81 per cent have crossed the graduation level.

Economic Profile

In respect of economic profile of priests at Tarakeswar, we consider two characteristics, (i) level of their income and (ii) family dependency ratio of priests. In terms of the economic variable, level of income, the priest households are classified into five categories. The income levels of priest families are examined as per capita income. The categories of per capita income of priest families are number of families belonging to per capita income of (i) Rs 500 and below (ii) Rs 501 to Rs 700, (iii) Rs 701 to Rs 900, (iv) Rs 901 to Rs 1000 and (v) Rs 1001 and above. Like the pilgrims' per capita income, the priest families' per capita income is measured by dividing total family income with the number of their family members. The percentage distribution of priest families according to the per capita level of income can be shown by the Table 12.

Table 12: Percentage Distribution of Priest Families according to the Level of their Per Capita Income

Level of Per Capita Income	*No. of Priest Families*	*Percentage No. to Total Sample*
Rs 500 and below	8	14.06
Rs 501-Rs 700	6	10.94
Rs 701-Rs 900	8	14.06
Rs 901-Rs 1000	16	28.13
Rs 1001 and above	18	32.81
Total	**56**	**100**

Source: Author's survey.

Table indicates that more 60 per cent (i.e., 60.94 per cent) families have per capita income of more than Rs 900. Among them, per capita income of Rs 1,000 is earned by 32.81 per cent families. Among the sample, 14.06 per cent families enjoy per capita income of below Rs 500 and Rs 701 to Rs 900 each. The lowest percentage (10.94 per cent) families earn the per capita income between Rs 701 and Rs 900. These figs imply that the economic condition of priest families is better at Tarakeswar. The attraction of deity of this place raises the congregation of pilgrims, which is one of the important reasons behind the better economic condition of priest families. Another reason is that among the sample, many priest families are the owner of rest houses. That is, they earn a lump-sum amount of money from this business along with their priest-craft profession.

Now, we discuss the economic condition of priest families by using another economic variable, namely family dependency ratio. By the family dependency ratio, we mean the determination of dependency by the non-working members to the total number of members in a family. The dependency enjoyed by the non-working members to the total members of sample priest families is measured by the family dependency ratio.

Family Dependency Ratio =

$$\frac{\text{No. of non - working members of the family}}{\text{Total no. of members of the family}}$$

Table 13: Percentage Distribution of Priest Families to Total Sample according to their Dependency Ratio

Family Dependency Ratio	*No. of Families*	*Percentage No. to Total Sample*
Below – .5	8	14.06
.5 – .7	19	34.38
.7 – .9	27	48.44
.9-1.0	2	3.12
Total	**56**	**100**

Source: Author's survey.

The family dependency ratios have been specified into four categories. The first category (below –.5) implies that 50 per cent or less number of non-working members of a family depends upon the working members. Similarly, the consecutive categories (.5-.7), (.7-.9) imply the 50 to 70 per cent, 70 to 90 per cent and 90-100 per cent dependency of the non-working family members, respectively. Table 13 indicates that among the 64 sample priest families, more than 50 per cent (i.e., 51.56 per cent) have greater dependency ratio. Table shows that 14.06 per cent families have minimum dependency, i.e., 50 per cent or less and only 3.12 per cent families have maximum dependency, i.e., 90 to 100 per cent. But 70 to 90 per cent dependency is going on maximum number of the priest families, i.e., on 48.44 per cent families to total sample. From this dependency table, we can say that there are greater dependencies on priesthood profession under sacred group at this pilgrimage centre.

By using these data, we can also construct the bi-variate data on priests. Percentage distribution of priests with different educational levels according their experience index are shown in Table 14.

Table 14: Percentage Distribution of Priests with Various Eperience Indexes according to their Level of Education

Education / Experience Index	*Below-10*	*10-20*	*20-30*	*30-40*	*40-50*	*50-60*	*60-70*	*70-80*	*80-100*
Upto Secondary level	3.6	7.1	10.7	17.86	14.3	10.7	14.3	10.7	10.7
Upto Higher Secondary level	13.3	13.3	20	6.7	20	6.7	0	13.3	6.7
Graduation and above	9.5	19	23.8	14.3	14.3	9.5	4.76	4.76	0

Source: Author's survey.

This table indicates that lower educated group have greater experience and higher educated group have comparatively lower experience. However, the 40 to 50 per cent experience is enjoyed by maximum priests with higher secondary and graduation level of education and 30 to 40 per cent experience is gained by the priests with secondary level of education.

The bi-variate data on family dependency ratio along with level of per capita income of sample priests are shown in Table 15

Table 15: Percentage Distribution of Priests with Various Dependency Ratios under Different Per Capita Income

Dependency Ratio / Income	*Below-500*	*501-700*	*701-900*	*901-1000*	*1001-above*
Below-.5	44.44	22.22	11.11	11.11	11.11
.6-.7	13.64	9.09	13.64	31.82	31.82
.8-.9	6.45	9.68	16.13	32.26	35.48
.9-1	0	0	0	0	100

Source: Author's survey.

This table represents that there is greater percentage of priests under lower income category having lower dependency. Similarly, more percentage numbers of priests under higher income groups having higher dependency. From this table, we get 44.44 per cent priests under lower income group have less than 50 per cent dependency and zero per cent has 90-100 per cent dependency under same income category. On the other hand, 35.48 per cent priests under higher income group having 80-90 per cent dependency. It implies that as family dependency increases, the per capita income also increases.

Under this sacred specialist, there is another group of religious agents, namely pilgrim guides. There are 280 registered pilgrim guides and many unregistered pilgrim guides, who maintain their livelihood by assigning in the worships and rites of devotees at this sacred centre, Tarakeswar. This number would increase from 400 to 500 at different auspicious seasons like *'Sravani Purnima'*, *'Chaitra Sankranti'* and also on Sunday, Monday and usual holidays. Like the priests, they are not employed by the Temple Estate Authority. But among them, all the registered pilgrim guides are associated with their union named *'Pradarsak Sangha'*, established in 1977. The registered pilgrim guides have their identity cards, issued by their union. Besides these, this organisation performs different types of welfare activities like donating books, money to various needy persons and also help their members by giving loans. The pilgrim guides earn a lump-sum amount of money by providing amenities to the pilgrims for fulfilling their religious requirements.

We have already discussed about the pilgrim guides in the earlier chapters. At Tarakeswar, pilgrim guides act as an intermediary between pilgrims and priests. There are three types of pilgrim guides. These are regular, casual and seasonal pilgrim guides. Most of the registered pilgrim guides fall under the first category, i.e., regular pilgrim guides, who work daily. They use to wait for catching the pilgrims at railway station, bus stand, and on the main road leading to the temple. The pilgrim guides under second category, i.e., casual pilgrim guides, do this work mainly on holidays and when they have to work on some one's behalf. The third category is of seasonal workers, who use to hunt for pilgrims only during different festive seasons, like *'Sravani Purnima'*, *'Chaitra Sankranti'*, *'Sivaratri'*, etc. Maximum number of casual and seasonal pilgrim guides is employed in permanent jobs elsewhere other than pilgrim hunting. The pilgrim guides not only come from local areas at Tarakeswar, but also hail from neighbouring villages and blocks. Mainly, a large number of regular and casual pilgrim guides come from local areas and the seasonal workers are from neighbouring villages and blocks. Specially on *'Sravani Purnima'*, many local and neighbouring village youths work as pilgrim guides at this pilgrimage centre.

Our investigation on the pilgrim guides indicates that on an average they earn a respectful amount of income from this profession. They earn revenues from different sources. For giving amenities to the pilgrims, they earn income as service charges from these pilgrims. Likewise, they adopt different strategies to extract money from various ritual and non-ritual functionaries like priests, florists, rest house owners, restaurant owners and so on. A large number of regular pilgrim guides work on contractual basis under different priests, rest house owners. For doing this, the pilgrim guides are given a lump-sum amount of money in advance by the priests and rest house owners. On the contrary, the casual and seasonal pilgrim guides and also some regular pilgrim guides earn a large amount of money as commission from the the priests and rest house owners to whom they provide the pilgrims. Our investigation shows that the pilgrim guides get 40 to 45 per cent share from priests and 25 to 30 per cent share from rest house owners. Therefore, the examination illuminates that most of the regular pilgrims depend economically on this sacred centre much more than the priests. They have no alternative sources of family income except pilgrim hunting. But the dimensions of economic sources for the subsistence of the casual and seasonal pilgrim guides are not only the deity of this pilgrimage place but also they are employed in agriculture, industry, business, service, etc.

Now, we examine another group, i.e., secular group of religious agents, at Tarakeswar. Like the sacred group, the secular group is also divided into two categories: (a) Permanent Employees, and (b) Temporary Employees. The permanent employees are employed by the Temple Estate Authority. Also the temporary employees are employed by the Estate Authority but not for throughout the year. They are appointed only for festive seasons like *'Sravani Purnima'*, *'Chaitra Sankranti'*, etc. That's why, the temporary employees are usually called seasonal employees.

Under permanent employees of Temple Estate Authority, there are different types of workers like accountant, estate manager, treasurer, surveyor, pundits, sweepers, scavengers, guards and some maid servants, who earn a fixed salary by providing different types of secular services to patronise the religious activities at Tarakeswar. There are one accountant, one manager, one treasurer, eight official clerks, two Sanskrit pundits, four cookers and helpers, one electrician, five staffs of miscellaneous works and market department, twenty one darwans (guards), eight sweepers and two servants appointed permanently by the Temple Estate Authority. Besides these, the Estate Authority also appoints five temporary staffs and five part-time staffs in the festive seasons for the convenience of the administrative activities. All the employees get regular salaries and along with it they also earn a lump-sum amount of money on the religious occasions. In the Temple Estate Authority, *Mohanta* is a highest paid employee getting Rs 3,500 (approximately) per month. The estate manger gets Rs 3,000 (approximately), the accountant gets Rs 2,700 (approximately) salary per month. The lowest paid workers are sweepers, guards, etc. getting Rs 1800 (approximately) per month. In the religious seasons, particularly certain departments are deriving various means to exploit the laxity of the administration for making an extra income.

Therefore, by facilitating the ritual performances at Tarakeswar to the devotees, the religious agents (i.e., both sacred and secular group) earn their subsistence to maintain their livelihood.

5.4 Local Hospitality Providers: Socio-economic Profile

Like the religious agents, there are other beneficiary associates at Tarakeswar, who provide various secular amenities and assisting the ritual worships and rites to the devotees directly in order to fulfill their religious needs.

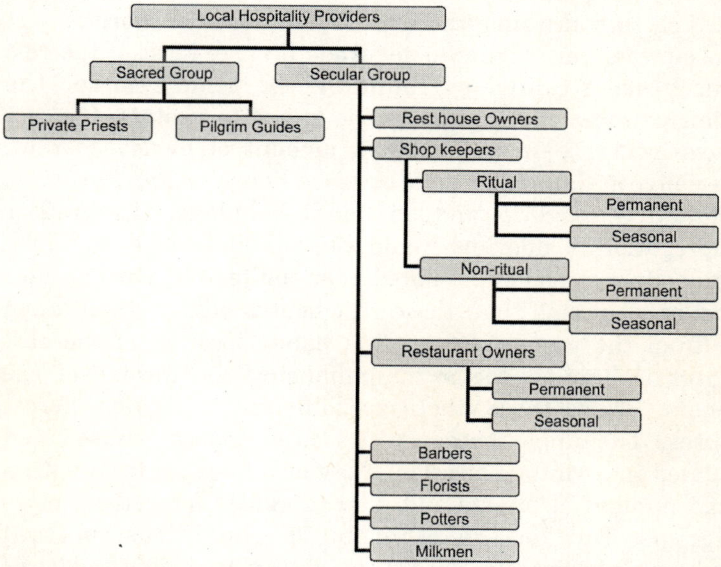

Fig. 12: Different Categories of Local Hospitality Providers.

These associates are called local hospitality providers. The break-up of local hospitality providers can be shown by the Fig. 12. This fig. shows that the local hospitality providers are divided into two groups: (1) Sacred group (2) Secular group. We have already discussed about the sacred group in the previous chapter. In this chapter, we discuss about only secular group. The secular group under local hospitality providers supplies those various non-ritual services to the devotees at this sacred centre which are essential for the religious activities. This group consists of rest house owners, shopkeepers, restaurant owners, barbers, florists, water carriers, potters and milkmen.

Our investigation shows that there are more or less 60 rest houses (including hotels and *'dharmashalas'*) at Tarakeswar. Among them, one is owned by Municipal Authority, named Municipality Guest House, one is government guest house and rests are private guest houses. Among these private rest houses, some (approximately four) *'dharmashalas'* are owned by different charitable trusts. Except these, among other private guest houses, six are government authorised, i.e., they have proper government trade license and rests have not, i.e., they are unauthorised. But these unauthorised rest house owners are trying to get trade license. Most of the rest houses are situated surrounding the temple under the municipal area. By hiring out the rooms to visitors, the rest house owners earn a lump-sum amount of money as rent. Specially, in different festive seasons like *'Sravani Purnima'*, *'Chaitra Sankranti'* and on usual holydays, the greater congregation of pilgrims would raise their income manifold. Again the rest houses, situated near the temple, earn greater amount of income than those rest houses which are situated far from the temple. Hence, the handy location of the rest houses is another factor for enhancing the income of the owners. Beside these, there are different categories of rest houses. The upper category possesses *'pucca'* houses and situated in a vintage position. They also have contacts with a large number of priests and pilgrim guides for getting more pilgrims. But on the other hand, the infrastructural arrangements, facilities are not satisfactory in middle and lower categories of rest houses. That's why, the income potentiality of those belonging to lower category is lesser than the earning potentiality of the upper class rest houses. Furthermore, many *'yatrinibas'* (rest house) have their own shops at which the owners sell the ritual articles like *'batasa'* (sweets), *'nakuldana'* (sweet), *'dala'* (a small basket made by clay containing offering to the deity), *'taga'* (an armlet), etc. to the pilgrims, who come and stay in these *'yatrinibas'* to mitigate their religious needs. By selling those ritual articles, the rest house owners earn a moderate income. Besides these, other members of most of the rest house owners' families are engaged with other sources of income. For example, many of them have chosen to be priest by services, pilgrim guide services, government or non-government services, etc.

People living at Tarakeswar and also far away from Tarakeswar derive economic benefits directly or indirectly from this religious establishment. The cult of *'Baba Taraknath'* helped develop a number of traders in the neighbourhood of the temple. These are shopkeepers, rest house owners. Considering the nature of their business, these are divided into two categories. Some of the traders provide services related with the deity and some are related with the non-ritual services. According to the time being devoted by them, the traders are also divided into two categories:, (1) Permanent and (2) Seasonal. Here we consider only those shops, restaurants, etc., which are situated in the temple premises and the surrounding areas of the temple.

Firstly, we discuss about those traders, who are related with the ritual performances. Under this category, we consider the sweetmeat shops, fruit shops, pilgrims-oriented articles such as *'dala'*, *'jal ghat',* etc. selling shops, etc. There are 30 shops of sweetmeats. Among them, eight are situated in the surrounding areas of the temple and rests are situated extent from the temple at Tarakeswar. Besides these, there are 20 shops selling fruits at this sacred centre. In the temple premises, there are 20 stalls, selling *'jal ghats'* (a small earthen or plastic vessels decorated with white flowers, garlands *'vilwa'* leaves, filled with the sacred water of *Ganga* and raw milk), white flowers (Calotropis Gigantia), garlands, sacred water of *'dudh pukur'* and *'taga'* (an armlet). There are also 40 shops of *'dala'* (a small earthen pot containing sweetmeats offering to the deity of *'Baba Taraknath'*) in both inside and outside of the temple premises. All these sellers, related with the religious practices of pilgrims, earn a good income to maintain their livelihood.

With these ritual associated shops, there are some other stores for selling non-ritual articles. Under this category, we consider those shops which are selling the stationary articles, images of different idols made of metal, stone and plastic clay, couch shells, photographs of different gods bordered with wooden frame, *'Mongal ghat'* (a consecrated pitcher placed for divine favour), toys, etc. Under this category, we also consider the different fruit pickles selling shops. Most of them are situated at temple adjoining areas. Approximately 32 stationary shops, 60 shops of photographs, toys, images of different gods, 24 shops of fruit pickle are situated in the wards four and five, which are the adjoining wards of the temple ward six. They all derive a steady income from their respective professions.

Now, we discuss another local hospitality provider that is restaurant owner. It includes all types of hotels for eating meals, restaurants for eating tiffin, snacks, etc. There are 42 restaurants at Tarakeswar. Most of the owners are from the local inhabitants of Tarakeswar. Some hotels among them are vegetarian. The majority of the restaurant owners are Bengalese, but there are some non-Bengali owners. All they earn a satisfactory income to maintain their subsistence level of living.

These two types of traders under secular group are also divided into two categories. The above figs. of the traders are all the permanent traders. But during some auspicious seasons like *'Sravani Purmima'*, *'Chaitra Sankranti'*, *'Sivaratri'* and usual holydays, the number would increase manifold due to the establishment of seasonal traders at Tarakeswar. The investigation shows that generally the number would increases to 3,500-4,000 on *'Sravani Purnima'*. The seasonal traders set up the temporary stalls in the temple ground, open space at the edge of the main road, in front of the main shops during the major festive occasions. During these auspicious seasons, they make fairly good earnings every year from Tarakeswar-bound pilgrims.

Moreover, there are many stalls in Sheraphuli, Baidyabati, Barakpur region, which sell the religious articles to both Tarakeswar-bound pilgrims as well as resident people. Compared to other stall owners, the stalls near the Nimai Tirtha Ghat earn a fairly high and steady income due to the vintage location of their shops and larger inflow of pilgrims to the sacred ghat (bank of river Ganga). Similarly, at Tarakeswar the traders near the temple earn larger income than others. In this way, the permanent and seasonal traders near and far away from Tarakeswar maintain their livelihood from the patronage of Temple of *'Baba Taraknath'*.

We make a field investigation on 85 traders under secular group of local hospitality providers. This investigation was undertaken on rest house owners, shopkeepers and restaurant owners. Like the priests at first, we determine the percentage distribution of local hospitality providers to total sample according to their Experience Index. The Experience Index can be measured by the following formula:

$$\text{Experience Index} = \frac{(\text{Observed value of working years} - \text{Minimum value of working years})}{(\text{Maximum value of working years} - \text{Minimum value of working years})} \times 100$$

Our examination shows that maximum value of experience of traders is 76 years and minimum value is 10 years. Using this formula of Experience Index on 85 samples, we get the following Table 16:

Table 16: Percentage Distribution of Providers to Total Sample according to their Experience Index

Experience Index (Percentage)	*No. of Providers*	*Percentage No. to Total Sample*
Below -10	9	8.24
10-20	12	10.59
20-30	11	9.41
30-40	9	8.24
40-50	19	16.47
50-60	22	18.82
60-70	12	10.59
70-80	9	8.23
80-100	11	9.41
Total	**115**	**100.00**

Source: Author's survey.

The experiences are divided from 10 to 100 per cent. Most of the hospitality providers of the sample fall in the groups, whose experiences are 40 to 50 V and 50 to 60 per cent experience. These are 16.47 per cent and 8.82 to total sample, respectively. The minimum percentage, i.e., 8.24, of traders have lower experience, i.e., 10 per cent. This percentage would also lay in the experience groups 30 to 40 per cent and 70 to 80 per cent. In total sample 9.41 V traders have both experience level 20 to 30 per cent and 80 to 100 per cent. Another larger percentage, i.e., 10.59, of traders have gained two experience level of 10 to 20 per cent and 60 to 70 per cent from their profession.

Any culture of a society is guided by the educational level of the community of that society. The educational level of the Local Hospitality Group is shown in Table 17:

Table 17: Percentage Distribution of Local Hospitality Providers according to their Educational Level

Educational Level	*No. of Providers*	*Percentage No. of Providers to Total Sample*
Upto Secondary Level	64	55.29
Upto Higher Secondary Level	31	27.06
Graduation and above	20	17.65
Total	**115**	**100**

Source: Author's survey.

This table indicates that more than 50 per cent providers have lower educational qualification. That is, 55.29 per cent providers to total sample come from the secondary educational level. Providers with the higher secondary educational level constitute 27.06 per cent and 17.65 per cent providers are from graduation or above category of education. So, the educational levels of local provider groups are more or less satisfactory.

We have already said that the various local hospitality providers like rest-house owners, shopkeepers, restaurant owners, etc. earn a satisfactory income to maintain their livelihood. The level of income of various providers is shown in Table 18.

Table 18: Percentage Distribution of Hospitality Providers as per their Level of Income

Level of Per Capita Income	*No. of Providers*	*Percentage No. of Providers to Total Sample*
Below – 500	9	8.24
501 – 700	15	12.94
701 – 900	38	32.94
901 – 1,000	31	27.06
1,001 – above	22	18.82
Total	**115**	**100**

Source: Author's survey.

Table illuminates that more than 20 per cent providers to total sample, i.e., 21.18 per cent, lies below the poverty line, i.e., they are lying below Rs 700 level of income. The highest percentage, i.e., 32.94, providers fall in the income group of Rs 701 to Rs 900. The highest income earners, i.e., Rs 1,001 and above constitutes 18.82 per cent providers and second highest percentage of local providers group, i.e., 27.06, of total sample fall in the income group of Rs 901 to Rs 1,000. These earnings do not come to the providers at the uniform pace. This is the measurement of average level of income throughout the year. Because they earn minimum income in the lean period and, on the other hand, in the auspicious seasons their income would increase manifold. So, the economic condition of the hospitality providers is fairly good in comparison to the earning of an average Indian.

Now, we consider the bi-variate data of local hospitality providers from Experience Index and the level of education is shown in Table 19.

Table 19: Percentage Distribution of Providers According to their Experience Index along with their Education Level

Level of Education / Experience Index (Percentage)	*Below-10*	*10-20*	*20-30*	*30-40*	*40-50*	*50-60*	*60-70*	*70-80*	*80-100*
Upto Secondary Education	2.13	4.25	8.51	6.38	21.3	23.4	14.9	8.51	10.6
Upto Higher Secondary Education	8.69	17.4	8.69	13.1	17.4	13.1	4.35	13.1	4.35
Graduation and above	26.67	20	13.3	6.67	0	13.3	6.67	0	13.3

Source: Author's survey.

This table represents that the maximum percentage of traders (23.40 per cent) with secondary level of education have 50 to 60 per cent experience in their profession. Very small percentage (i.e., 2.13 per cent) of providers with same educational qualification have small experience that is less than 10 per cent experience level and the higher experience level, i.e., more than 80 per cent are gained by 10.64 per cent of total providers with secondary education level. Similarly, in the total sample traders with higher secondary level of education, 17.39 per cent have both 10 to 20 per cent and 40 to 60 per cent experience. But the highest experience (i.e., more than 80 per cent) is enjoyed by only 4.35 per cent providers and the minimum experience level (i.e., less than 10 per cent) is acquired by a little better percentage, i.e., 8.69, of total providers. On the contrary, the maximum providers (26.67 per cent) with higher educational qualification, graduation and above, have little experience, i.e., less than 10 per cent in their profession and the maximum experience is obtained by 13.33 per cent providers under the same level of education. This table implies that there is a greater attachment of lower educated people than higher educated people with their profession.

Now we consider another relation between level of income with the level of education of the sample traders. The bi-variate data can be shown by Table 20.

Table 20: Percentage Distribution of Providers under Different Education Levels according to their Level of Income

Level of Education / Level of Income	*Below – 500*	*501 – 700*	*701 – 900*	*901 – 1,000*	*1,001 – above*
Upto Secondary Level	10.64	17.02	29.79	27.66	14.89
Upto Higher Secondary Education	8.7	8.7	39.13	21.74	21.74
Graduation and above	0	6.67	33.33	33.33	26.67

Source: Author's survey.

Table exhibits that the maximum percentages of total providers, i.e., 29.79 per cent, under secondary level of education have per capita income of Rs 701 to Rs 900. Under the same educational qualification, the minimum percentage, i.e., 10.64 per cent, of providers have lower level of income, i.e., less than Rs 500 and maximum income Rs 1001 and above is earned by the 14.89 per cent providers. Likewise, the maximum percentage, 39.13, of total providers with the higher secondary level of education has income Rs 701 to Rs 900. Under the same educational qualification, the minimum percentage, i.e., 8.7, of providers have income of Rs 500 and below and maximum income of Rs 1001 and above is earned by 21.74 per cent providers. Under higher level of education, i.e., graduation and above, the maximum percentage, i.e., 33.33, of providers also have income of Rs 701 to Rs 900. But under this educational category, there are no providers with income of Rs 500 and less and 26.67 per cent providers enjoy highest level of income. The discussion indicates that most of the providers with lower level of education have satisfactory level of income and most providers from all levels of education have concentrated around the income level of Rs 701 to Rs 900.

Like the priests, here we also consider the dependency ratio of families of local hospitality provider groups. This is measured by number of non-working family members to total number of members of that family. This can be shown in the following way:

Family Dependency Ratio =

$$\frac{\text{Number of non working members}}{\text{Total number of family members}} \times 100 .$$

The percentage of family dependency of various providers are shown in Table 21.

Table 21: Percentage Distribution of Providers to Total Sample according to their Family Dependency Ratio

Family Dependency Ratio (Percentage)	*No. of Providers*	*Percentage No. to the Total Sample*
Below – 50	8	7.06
50 – 70	53	45.88
70 – 90	38	32.94
90 – 100	16	14.12
Total	**115**	**100**

Source: Author's survey.

This Table 21 indicates that the highest percentage, i.e., 45.88, of local hospitality providers to total sample have 50 to 70 per cent family dependency ratio. The minimum dependency ratio, i.e., 50 or less would lay on 7.06 per cent providers and maximum dependency ratio, i.e., 90 to 100, lie on smaller percentage of providers, i.e., 14.12. It implies greater families of providers at Tarakeswar have 50 to 90 per cent dependency of non-working people to total family.

Now, under different income groups how the family dependency ratio can fluctuate, is examined by Table 22.

This table displays that the maximum percentage of family dependency ratio of traders would take place in lower income group of Rs 500 and less.

Table 22: Percentage Distribution of Providers with Family Dependency Ratio under Different Income Categories

Dependency Ratio / Income	*Below - 500*	*501-700*	*701-900*	*901-1,000*	*1,001-above*
Below – 50	50	16.67	33.33	0	0
60 – 70	5.13	17.95	38.46	25-64	12.82
80 – 90	3.57	7.14	21.43	32.14	35.71
90 – 100	8.33	8.33	41.67	33.33	8.35

Source: Author's survey.

Under the higher income group of Rs 1,001 and above, the family dependency ratio is nil. The percentages of traders is maximum (i.e., 35.71) under higher income groups which have greater dependency ratio of 80 to 90 per cent. The maximum dependency would take place in 41.67 per cent providers, which are lying under middle income group (i.e., Rs 701-900). Besides these, 38.46 per cent providers under middle income group (i.e., Rs 701-900) have 60 to 70 per cent dependency. This table usually implies that as dependency ratio increases then income of that family also increases. In this way, we can discuss about the socio-economic profile of rest house owners, shopkeepers and restaurant owners as a whole.

Along with these hospitality groups, there are some other categories of providers like barbers, florists, potters, milkmen. They all earn a satisfactory level of income to maintain their subsistence of living by providing various services to the visitors at Tarakeswar to fulfill their requirements conveniently. They all are privately employed at the tonsuring centre of the temple as they are directly associated with this sacred zone of Tarakeswar. They work at this sacred centre on a co-operative basis. Some barbers are associated with the different priests and pilgrim guides on contractual basis. On the other hand, the potters have a fixed set of clients like tea stalls, sweetmeat shops, hotels, restaurants, rest houses, etc. where their commodities are used. Likewise, the florists run their business on co-operative basis within the same occupational groups by joining with the pottery dealers, sacred water dealers and milkmen and, in the same way, the milkmen supply milk to the various tea stalls, sweetmeat shops and households. They are also related with the florists to prepare some religious articles like *'jal ghat'*, *'ghat',* etc. They also supply milk to the temple for religious purposes. Throughout the year, especially in the auspicious seasons, they earn a good income to maintain their livelihood.

Therefore, it is clear that the deity of *'Baba Taraknath'* at Tarakeswar provides the employment facilities directly or indirectly to the people, under diverse occupational groups.

5.5 Analysis

In this section, we discuss about the socio-economic profile of pilgrims, temple employees and the local hospitality providers consecutively. It is the first micro-based analysis of this project. How the non-economic factor, religious culture, affects the social, economic and cultural state of Tarakeswar is examined by micro-level analysis in this chapter. Firstly, we examine the socio-economic nature of pilgrims from different aspects, by using different types of frequency curves, bar diagrams and pie charts. Secondly, we examine the socio-economic conditions of different temple employees and, finally, we discuss about local hospitality providers from similar aspects by using different types of frequency curves.

A continuous frequency distribution, associated with a large number of cases, the date may be divided into small class intervals, so that the magnitude of class frequencies is fluctuated with the increase in the number of classes. This would cause many small rectangles of a histogram, when the dates are plotted on the graph. Thus, when a frequency polygon is drawn through the tops of these columns, it would appear almost like a smooth mathematical curve. Therefore, for a continuous distribution related to a large number of observations, a smooth frequency curve may be drawn, that represents the distribution. Besides this, the smooth frequency curve can be used with continuous data only and the graphic method is similar with the frequency polygon and it may be drawn smoothly without drawing the histogram. In case of frequency curve, there is no limitation of specific class intervals.

In our analysis, we use various types of frequency curves like normal frequency curve, positively and negatively skewed frequency curve, J-shaped frequency curve, multimodal frequency curve, etc. Now we analyse the socio-economic nature of the members of the society related with this particular religious culture.

(A) Analysis of Socio-economic Features of Pilgrims

In order to examine the socio-economic nature, we made a field investigation at Tarakeswar on different periods of time. The data collected from the sample of 733 pilgrims at railway station, bus stop, rest houses, etc. at random by using structured and open-ended questionnaire schedules. Only the adult pilgrims, aged 20 or more, were surveyed. The sample individuals were selected on the basis of inflow and outflow of pilgrims into the temple or at some other places they halted. The socio-economic, religious and other related information like place of origin, demographic particularities, relationship with temple, numbers of visits, per capita income, about the religious and non-religious services they obtained from the priests, pilgrim guides, local hospitality providers, municipality, etc., occupation, expenditure to fulfill their religious requirements, whether get religious satisfaction or not, etc. From the sample pilgrims, the data were collected by interview and the data relating to the act of pilgrimage activities were collected through systematic observation of the pilgrims' behaviour.

To examine the socio-economic nature of the pilgrims, we consider four types of bi-variate data of socio-economic factors and these are represented by the concerned frequency curve diagrams. These are given below.

The figs. under bi-variate data represent that among all other districts the maximum percentage of pilgrims with per capita income of Rs 1001 and above comes from the capital city of Kolkata. It also exhibits that the greater percentage of lower income earning pilgrims comes from rural areas as compared to other areas and the greater percentage of higher income pilgrims comes from urban areas. Another phenomenon is that, except Kolkata, in every district, most of the pilgrims come from the per capita income level of Rs 701-900. The percentage attendance of pilgrims from higher income group is higher than the pilgrims from lower income groups due to bad financial condition of the poor.

Now, we consider Fig. 13, which represents that most of the pilgrims come from West Bengal to Tarakeswar. That is, there is a regional importance of the sacred place in India.

Table 23: No. of Pilgrims from Different States

Area of Origin State	*No. of Pilgrims*
West Bengal	715
Bihar	2
Jharkhand	8
Orissa	6
Assam	2

Source: Author's survey.

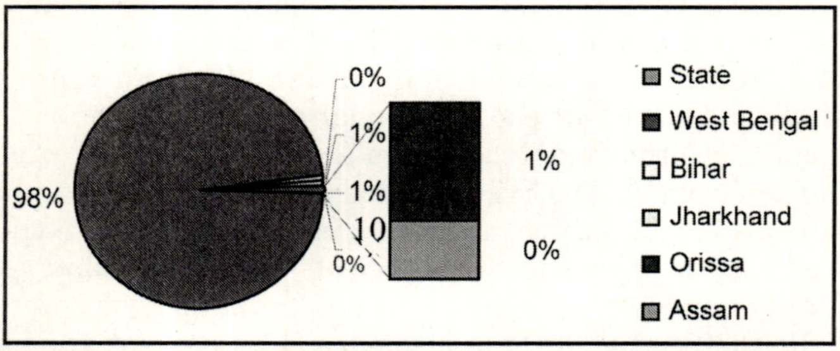

Fig. 13. Percentage No. of Pilgrims from Different States.

Visits of pilgrims from different districts in West Bengal are shown in Fig. 14.

Table 24: No. of Pilgrims from Different Districts of West Bengal

Districts	*No. of Pilgrims*
Kolkata	161
Howrah	125
Hooghly	73
Burdwan	66
Bankurah	7
Birbhum	22
Nadia	29
Mursidabad	22
North 24-Parganas	37
South 24-Parganas	51
Midnapur	132
Purulia	7

Source: Author's survey.

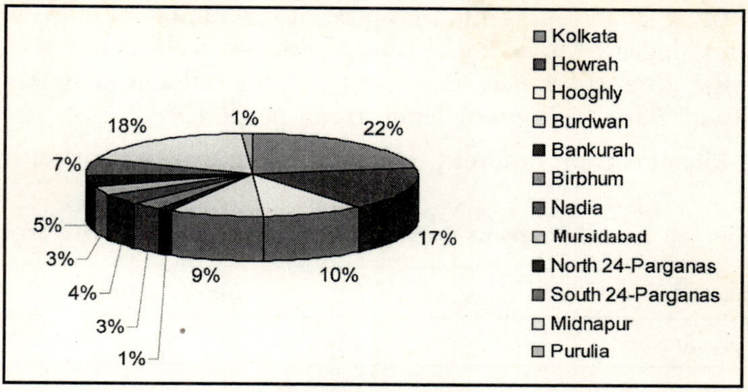

Fig. 14

Fig. 14 represents that among all districts the percentage visit by the pilgrims from Kolkata is higher than all other districts. Due to the improvement in communication system greater pilgrims come to Tarakeswar from neighbouring areas.

Visits of pilgrims from city, town and villages to Tarakeswar are shown in Fig. 15.

Table 25: No. of Pilgrims from Cities, Towns and Villages

Sector of Origin	*No. of Pilgrims*
Cities	220
Towns	191
Villages	322

Source: Author's survey.

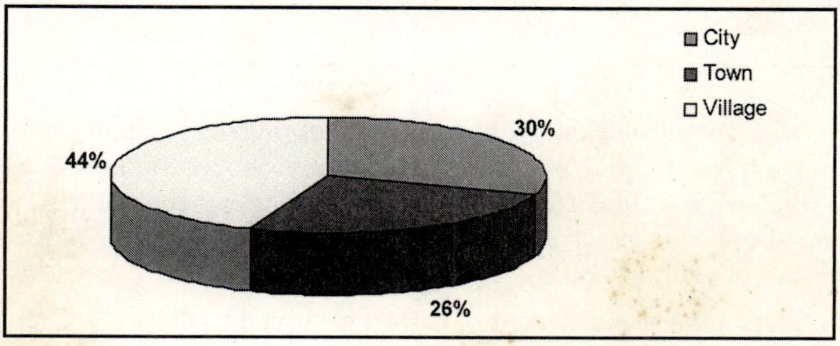

Fig. 15

But Fig. 15 represents that percentage number of pilgrims from villages is higher than that of cities as well as towns. It implies that rural people are very much influenced by the deity of *'Baba Taraknath'* than urban people.

Pilgrims from different occupational groups are shown in Fig. 16.

Table 26: No. of Pilgrims from Different Occupation Structures

Occupation	*No. of Pilgrims*
Agriculture	44
Business	191
Government Services	66
Non-government Services	161
Menial Works	117
Other Works	154

Source: Author's survey.

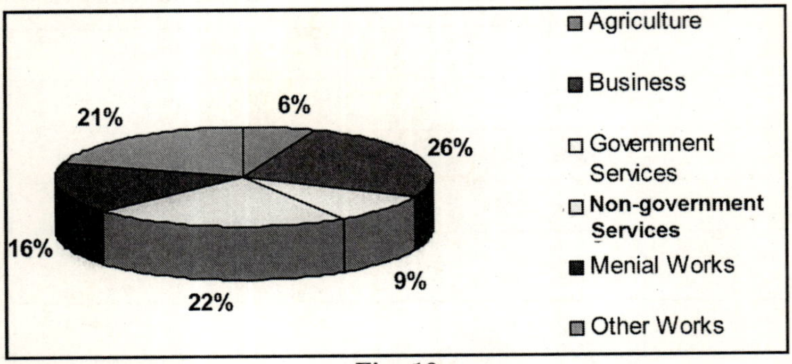

Fig. 16

Fig. 16 shows that greater number of pilgrims comes from business sector and non-government services. It implies due to the greater uncertainty in their profession, the pilgrims from business sector and non-government sector come more to this pilgrimage place.

Pilgrims from different earnings groups are shown in Fig, 17. It implies that the congregations of middle income earning class of pilgrims visit more than other income earning groups.

Table 27: No. of Pilgrims under Different Monthly Per Capita Income Groups

Monthly Per Capita Income	*No. of Pilgrims*
Below-500	66
501-700	88
701-900	279
901-1,000	81
1,001-above	220

Source: Author's survey.

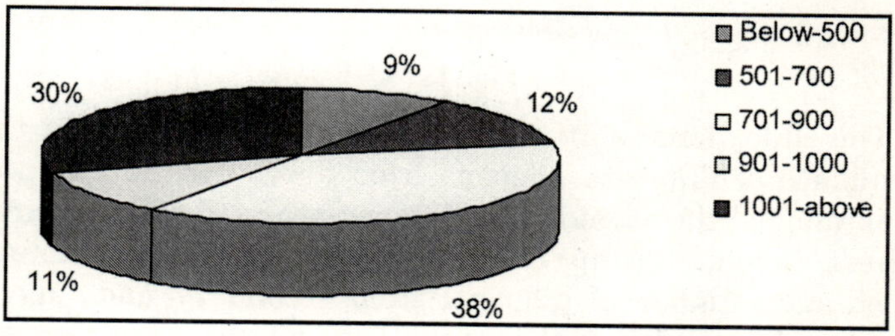

Fig. 17

Then we look at the percentages of pilgrims under different income groups from different sectors of origin like city, town and village, shown in Fig. 18 that represents the greater percentage of pilgrims of higher income groups comes from cities as well as towns compared to villages.

Table 28: Percentage Distribution of Pilgrims from Different Sectors according to their Per Capita Income Groups

Per Capita Income / Sector of Origin	*Percentage No. of Pilgrims Coming from Cities*	*Percentage No. of Pilgrims Coming from Towns*	*Percentage No. of Pilgrims Coming from Villages*
Below-500	4.598	8	13.28
501-700	5.75	14.7	15.6
701-900	28.74	52	35.94
901-1,000	16.09	10.7	7.03
1,001-Above	44.83	14.7	28.13

Source: Author's survey.

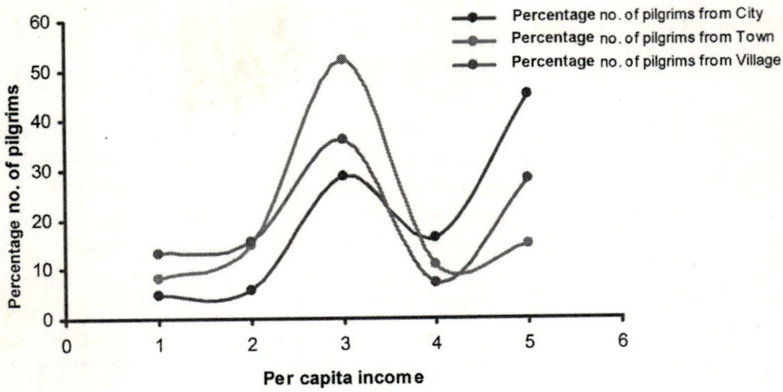

Fig. 18.

The educational status of sample pilgrims shows that the attendance of illiterate pilgrims from lower income group is maximum and the attendance of higher educated pilgrims from highest income group is maximum. But the maximum percentage number of pilgrims from secondary and higher secondary levels of education comes from middle income group. It implies that the glory of the deity of *'Baba Taraknath'* spread out among all levels of income earning groups as per their educational level. This is shown in Fig. 19.

Table 29: Percentage Distribution of Pilgrims with Different Levels of Education according to their Per Capita Income Groups

Per Capita Income / Education	*Percentage No. of Pilgrims without Education*	*Percentage No. of Pilgrims with Secondary Level of Education*	*Percentage No. of Pilgrims with Higher Secondary Level of Education*	*Percentage No. of Pilgrims with Graduation and Above*
Below-500	45	9.3	5.08	3.66
501-700	35	15.5	5.08	7.32
701-900	15	52.7	45.76	14.63
901-1,000	5	7.75	25.42	6.1
1,001-Above	0	14.7	18.64	68.29

Source: Author's survey.

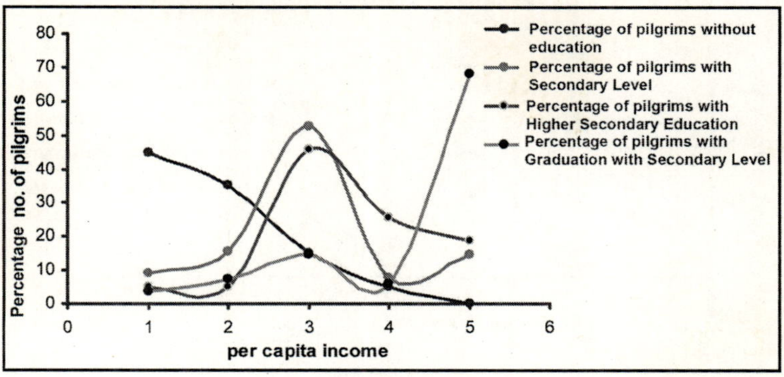

Fig. 19

The occupational structure of the pilgrims according to their per capita income represents that the percentage attendance of pilgrims under the middle income group is related with agriculture, business, non-government services and menial activities. In this income group, the attendance of pilgrims associated with the government activities is lower. This implies that, due to the uncertainty in this income group, the people related with agriculture, business, non-government activities and menial works are very much dependent on the deity and due to the more certainty the influence of deity is little lower on the people related with government activities. This is shown in Fig. 20.

Table 30: Percentage Distribution of Pilgrims Related to Different Occupational Structures according to their Per Capita Income Groups

Per Capita Income / Occupation	*Percentage No. of Pilgrims Related with Agriculture*	*Percentage No. of Pilgrims Related with Business*	*Percentage No. of Pilgrims Related with Govt. Activities*	*Percentage No. of Pilgrims Related with Non-Govt. Activities*	*Percentage No. of Pilgrims Related with Menial Activities*	*Percentage No. of Pilgrims Related with Other Activities*
Below-500	16.67	6.67	0	3.08	23.91	10
501-700	22.22	5.33	0	12.31	32.61	8.33
701-900	38.89	41.33	26.92	53.85	21.74	33.33
901-1,000	5.56	9.33	46.2	7.69	8.7	3.33
1,001-Above	16.67	37.33	26.92	23.08	13.04	45

Source: Author's survey.

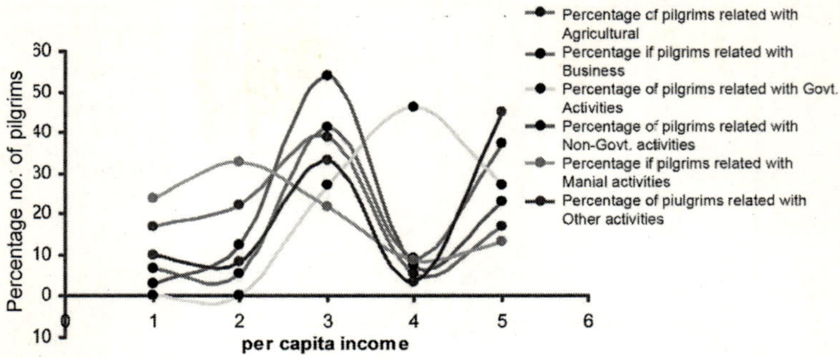

Fig. 20

Now, we consider the degree of devotion of different pilgrims under different income groups. The degree of devotion of pilgrims can be measured from the expenditure of the pilgrims for devotion. We can determine it by dividing total cost for devotion by the total income of that pilgrim. As per

Table 31: Percentage Distribution of Pilgrims under Different Income Groups according to their Degree of Devotion

Degree of Devotion / Income	*Below – 500*	*501-700*	*701-900*	*901-1,000*	*1,001-Above*
.02-.05	33.33	25.00	30.91	25.81	25.58
.06-.1	25.93	27.78	21.82	22.58	17.44
.11-.15	14.81	22.22	10.91	29.03	13.95
.16-.2	7.41	8.33	10.00	6.45	11.63
.21-.25	3.70	2.78	5.45	6.45	6.98
.26-.3	3.70	5.56	4.55	3.23	3.49
.31-.35	3.70	2.78	3.64	0.00	3.49
.36-.4	3.70	2.78	1.82	3.23	2.33
.41-.45	0.00	2.78	1.82	3.23	2.33
.46-.5	3.70	0.00	3.64	0.00	4.65
.51-.55	0.00	0.00	1.82	0.00	1.16
.56-.6	0.00	0.00	0.00	0.00	1.16
.61-.7	0.00	0.00	0.91	0.00	1.16
.71-.75	0.00	0.00	1.82	0.00	1.16
.76-.8	0.00	0.00	0.91	0.00	3.49

Source: Author's survey.

different per capita incomes, the percentage attendance of pilgrims with different degrees of devotion can be shown by Fig. (21). The degree of devotion of percentage of pilgrims with the group .02-.05 and .06-.1 are dominating under all income groups, except income group of Rs 901 to Rs 1000, compared to other groups of degree of devotion. On an average, the high income groups have greater degree of devotion than lower income groups. Although some groups with degree of devotion like .06-.1, .11-.15, .26-.3, .31-.35 and .36-.4 dominates higher income groups. Due to worse economic condition, the lower earning groups can afford the devotion expenditure where as higher income group can. The same phenomenon is shown in other income groups.

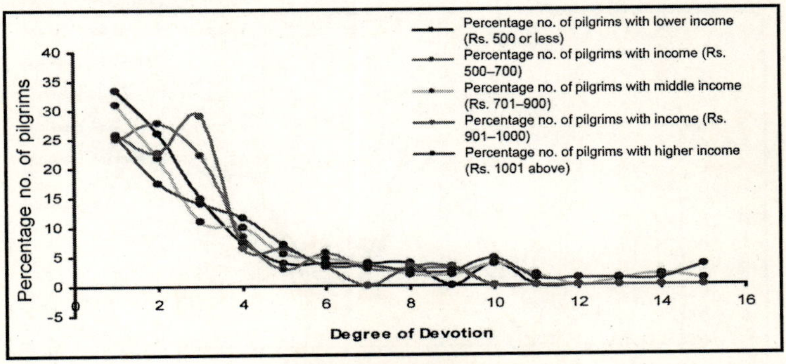

Fig. 21

Now, the efficiency to visit Tarakeswar by the pilgrims under different income groups are shown by in Fig. 22. Visit efficiency of pilgrims can be determined by dividing the number of visits with the maximum number of visits by the pilgrims. The fig. represents that in every visit efficiency category, the higher income earning pilgrims' attendance is higher than lower income groups, due to the satisfactory earnings. But the percentage number of attendance of pilgrims under different visit efficiencies is highest for the income group of Rs 701 to Rs 900.

Table 32: Percentage Distribution of Pilgrims with Different Experience Level as Per Capita Income

Income/Efficiency to visit	*.04-.2*	*.24-.4*	*.44-.6*	*.64-.8*	*.84-1*
Below - 500	10.13	9.46	7.14	5.88	7.69
501-700	13.92	10.81	3.57	17.65	15.38
701-900	33.54	43.24	46.43	41.18	38.46
901-1,000	12.03	6.76	10.71	17.65	7.69
1,001 - Above	30.38	29.73	32.14	17.65	30.77

Source: Author's survey.

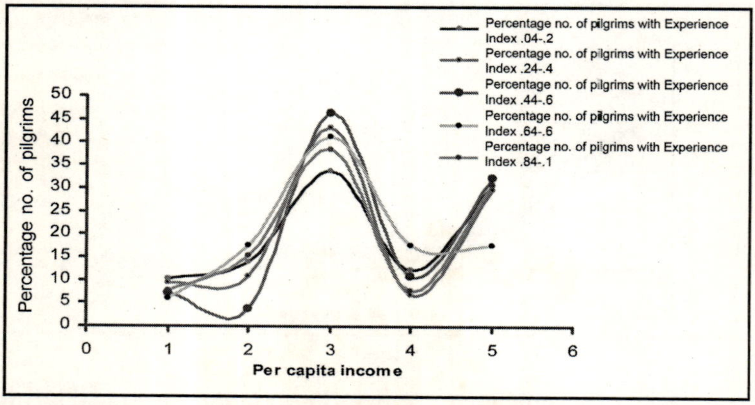

Fig. 22. Frequency Curve of percentage No. of Pilgrims with different experience level as per capita income.

Finally, to measure the inequality in income, we use the Elteto-Frigyes Measure. This measure shows by the formula, i.e.,

$$\text{Elteto-Frigyes Index (V)} = \frac{\text{Highest Value of Income}}{\text{Lowest Value of Income}}.$$

The calculation of this Index on 733 number of pilgrims' income is shown in the following Table 33.

Table 33: Elteto-Frigyes Index of Different Income Groups of Pilgrims

Income Group	*E-F Index*
V_1	3.18
V_2	1.15
V_3	4.09
V_4	1.33

Source: Author's calculation.

This table represents that income inequality is greater in lower income group (V_1) and middle income group (V_2).

(2) Analysis of Socio-economic Nature of Priests

The second stage of field work was conducted among the priests as the temple employees. Like the first stage of field work among the pilgrims, here we also collected data from the priests by using structured and open-ended questionnaire through interview method. The information was taken about their number, lineage, domicile, length of priesthood and also the genealogical information like kinship, marriage, migration, education, occupation, etc. The quantitative data about income, land holding, etc. was also collected from sample priests through interview at random. Besides these, the economic interactions among various temple employees and with the pilgrims were obtained from observational method. In our survey, we collected such information by interviewing 56 priests at random in this sacred centre. Now, we analyse the results obtained from the information by frequency curve.

Among different socio-economic factors, firstly we consider the educational status of priests under different income groups. The income is considered as per capita income determined by dividing total family income of the priests with their family members. The concerned frequency curve derived from the information is shown in Fig. 23. The level of income under all educational categories is quite better. The percentage number of priests with lower educational level has greater amount of lower level of income and the priests with higher level of education have higher level of income.

Table 34: Percentage Distribution of Priests with Different Levels of Education According to their Per Capita Income

Income/Education Level	*Percentage No. of Priests to Total under Secondary Level of Education*	*Percentage No. of Priests to Total under Higher Secondary Level of Education*	*Percentage No. of Priests to Total with Graduation and Above Level of Education*
Below-500	17.86	6.67	14.29
501-700	10.71	6.67	14.29
701-900	14.29	13.33	14.29
901-1,000	25	40	23.81
1,001-Above	32.14	13.33	33.33

Source: Author's survey.

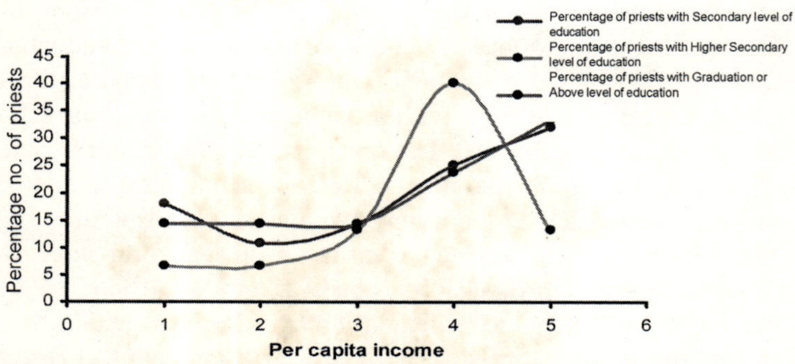

Fig. 23. Frequency Curve of percentage No. of Priests with Different Levels of Education According to their Per Capita Income.

Now, we consider the experience pattern of the priests. This can be determined by experience index of priests. Fig. 24 represents the percentage number of priests under various educational levels having different average experience in their profession. The fig. exhibits that the priests with low educational category have greater experience and the priests with higher education have lower experience level.

Table 35: Percentage Distribution of Priests with Different Levels of Education According to their Experience Index

Level of Education / Experience Index (average)	*Percentage No. of Priests to Total under Secondary Level of Education*	*Percentage No. of Priests to Total under Higher Secondary Level of Education*	*Percentage No. of Priests to Total under Graduation or Above Level of Education*
5	3.57	13.33	9.52
15	7.14	13.33	19
25	10.71	20	23.81
35	17.86	6.67	14.29
45	14.29	20	14.29
55	10.71	6.67	9.52
65	14.29	0	4.76
75	10.71	13.33	4.76
90	10.71	6.67	0

Source: Author's survey.

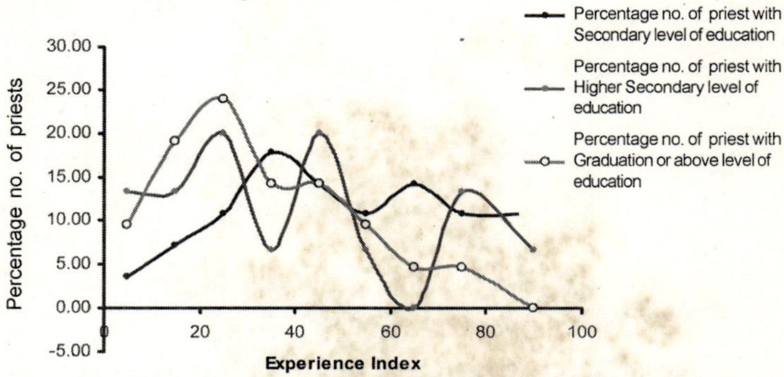

Fig. 24: Frequency Curve of Percentage No. of Priests with Different Levels of Education according their Experience Index.

The economic condition of the priests can be ascertained by the family dependency ratio. It is determined by dividing non-working members by total number of members of the priest's family. This is represented by Fig. 25. It reflects that priests under higher income group have higher dependency and under the lower income group have lower dependency. It follows the 'Chayanov Thesis' that as family dependency ratio increases then in order to raise the productivity the income will increase and mitigate the greater family dependency.

Table 36: Percentage Distribution of Priests with Different Dependency Levels according to their Per Capita Income

Dependency Ratio/Level of Income	*Percentage No. of Priest Dependency Ratio 50% and Below*	*Percentage No. of Priest Dependency Ratio 50 to 70%*	*Percentage No. of Priest Dependency Ratio 70 to 90%*	*Percentage No. of Priest Dependency Ratio 90 to 100%*
Below-500	44.44	13.64	6.45	0
501-700	22.22	9.09	9.68	0
701-900	11.11	13.64	16.13	0
901-1,000	11.11	31.82	32.26	0
1,001-Above	11.11	31.82	35.48	100

Source: Author's survey.

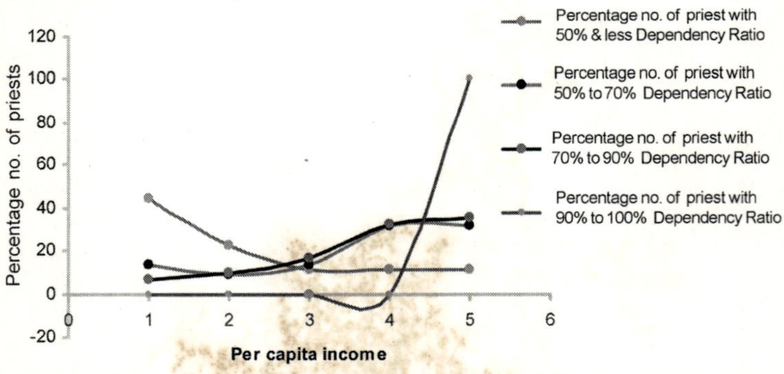

Fig. 25: Frequency Curve of Percentage No. of Priests with Different Dependency Level According to Level of Per Capita Income.

(3) Analysis of Socio-economic Nature of Local Hospitality Providers

In the same way, the third stage field investigation would take place on the local hospitality provider groups. Under this group, we collected data from rest houses, shopkeepers and restaurant owners. In all, a total number of 115 providers were surveyed at this sacred town. The data was collected about educational status, migration, occupational structure, number of earning members through interviewing the local providers. About the business establishment, investments, earnings are also collected by interview method. The analyses are represented by consecutive figs. given below.

The educational status of providers under different income groups can be represented by Fig. 26. It shows that higher educated providers earn higher income compared to others and lower educated providers have lower income. But the concentration of providers under income group of Rs 701 to Rs 900 is maximum than others at all educational categories. So, the economic condition of the local provider groups is roughly satisfactory.

Table 37: Percentage Distribution of Providers under Different Levels of Education according to their Per Capita Income

Level of Education / Income Level	*Percentage No. of Providers to Total under Secondary Level of Education*	*Percentage No. of Providers to Total under Higher Secondary Level of Education*	*Percentage No. of Providers to Total with Graduation and Above Level of Education*
Below-500	10.64	8.7	0
501-700	17.02	8.7	6.67
701-900	29.79	39.13	33.33
901-1,000	27.66	21.74	33.33
1,001-Above	14.89	21.74	26.67

Source: Author's survey.

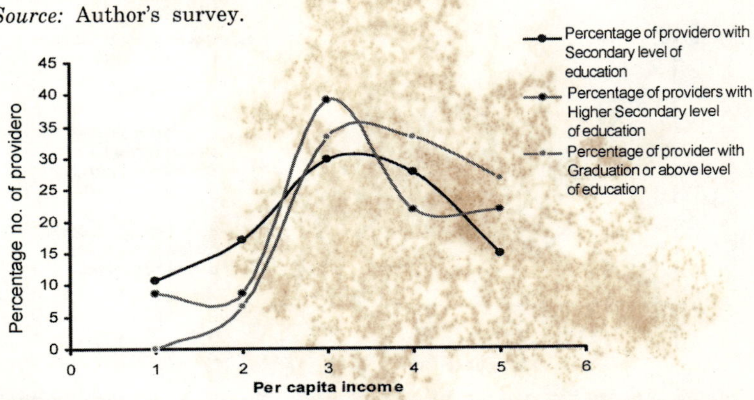

Fig. 26: Frequency Curve of Percentage No. of Providers under Different Level of Education according to their Per Capita Income.

Like the priests, we will measure the experience index of providers shown in Fig. 27. It also represents that the experience level of lower educated group is greater than the experience level of higher educated group.

Table 38: Percentage No. of Providers under Different Levels of Education according to their Experience Index

Level of Education\ Experience Index (average)	*Percentage No. of Providers to Total under Secondary Level of Education*	*Percentage No. of Providers to Total under Higher Secondary Level of Education*	*Percentage No. of Providers to Total under Graduation or Above Level of Education*
5	2.13	8.69	26.67
15	4.25	17.39	20
25	8.51	8.69	13.33
35	6.38	13.06	6.67
45	21.28	17.39	0
55	23.4	13.04	13.33
65	14.9	4.35	6.67
75	8.51	13.04	0
90	10.64	4.35	13.33

Source: Author's survey.

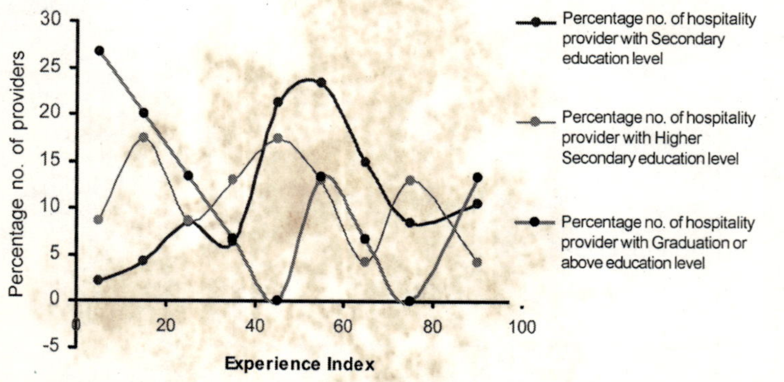

Fig. 27: Frequency Curve of Percentage No. of Providers under Different Levels of Education According to their Experience Index.

Finally, we examine the dependency ratio of local providers shown in Fig. 28. This fig. represents that except the providers with lower dependency ratio, the all sample providers under different dependency ratios raise with the rise in income. It roughly follows the Chayanov's Thesis, that is, the income level will increase with the increase in dependency ratio.

Table 39: Percentage Distribution of Providers under Different Dependency Ratios according to their Per Capita Income

Dependency Level / Level of Income	*Percentage No. of Providers Depend-ency Ratio 50% and Below*	*Percentage No. of Providers Dependency Ratio 50 to 70%*	*Percentage No. of Providers Dependency Ratio 70 to 90%*	*Percentag e No. of Providers Depende-ncy Ratio 90 to 100%*
Below-500	50	5.13	3.57	8.33
501-700	16.67	17.95	7.14	8.33
701-900	33.33	38.46	21.43	41.67
901-1,000	0	25.64	32.14	33.33
1,001-Above	0	12.82	35.71	8.33

Source: Author's survey.

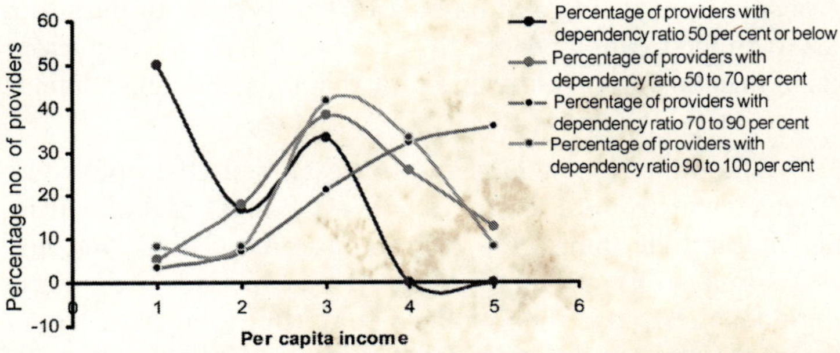

Fig. 28: Frequency Curve of Percentage No. of Providers under Different Dependency Ratios according to their Per Capita Income.

In this way, we can shortly analyse the socio-economic nature of ritual and non-ritual associates, who can earn their livelihood by providing different services to the devotees at this sacred town of Tarakeswar.

5.6 Conclusion

The examination of the socio-economic-cultural features of pilgrims' ritual and non-ritual associates on the basis of field investigation explores the socio-economic importance of the Religious Culture to the Human Culture. The micro-level analysis of the primary data obtained from field investigation on pilgrims, priests and local hospitality providers exhibits that how much they are guided by the particular Religious Culture, i.e., Temple Cultural, from their own socio-economic background. Actually, the socio-economic backgrounds of Tarakeswar and the devotees are very much steered by the temple of *'Baba Taraknath'*. In this chapter, we are sliding up this conclusion from previous discussion.

Tarakeswar is a smallest town under Hooghly District in West Bengal. But this place is lighted by the glory of *'Baba Taraknath'* to all devotees, living in our country and also in abroad. The town of Tarakeswar, without establishment of temple of *'Baba Taraknath'*, leaves nearly nothing. Due to the improvement of transport system, many people come to this place from various socio-economic backgrounds from different areas that generate greater economic activities which assist the people from inside and outside of Tarakeswar to maintain their livelihood. Many people at Tarakeswar earn a satisfactory level of income by providing different religious and non-religious services to the pilgrims.

The field survey on pilgrims represents that people come to Tarakeswar from all districts of West Bengal and also from other states like Jharkhand, Bihar, Assam, Odisha. Not only that, some pilgrims also come from abroad, i.e., from Bangladesh. So, the figs. explore that the nobility of *'Baba Taraknath'* crosses the regional boundary to all directions of India. However, due to the better communication system, a greater portion of the pilgrims come from neighbouring districts of Tarakeswar. The greater percentages of pilgrims come from Kolkata, Hooghly, Howrah, Burdwan. They also come from Midnapur, although, it is not the adjacent district of Tarakeswar. The fig. also represents that most of the pilgrims from better economic condition usually come from cities and towns, whereas the pilgrims from lower income groups come from village areas, although most of the pilgrims of the sample come from villages. So, there is a biasness of the rural people from any income groups for the deity than the urban people. The investigation on pilgrims shows that most of the pilgrims come from general castes and some come from other castes like scheduled castes and scheduled tribes. As per Hindu scriptures, it is an expecting feature. About the educational status, the survey represents that most of the pilgrims come to Tarakeswar from lower educational category. But the figs. from higher educational groups are not bad. If we consider the educational level along with the level of per capita income of the pilgrims, it is seen that higher income earning people come from higher educational group and vice versa. Yet maximum numbers of pilgrims with any educational qualification come from middle income group. Data on occupational structure of pilgrims exhibit that most of the pilgrims come from the occupation of business and the non-government services. But the attendance of pilgrims from agriculture and government sector is lower. It implies that due to uncertainty in their profession, the attendance of business persons and non-government service men is greater than that of the pilgrims from other profession.

The investigation on devotion expenditure by the pilgrims represents those pilgrims with lower income having greater amount of lower degree of devotion due to lack of financial assistance than middle and higher income groups. On the other hand, the pilgrims with higher income having greater amount of high degree of devotion than middle and lower income earning pilgrims due to greater financial strength. It implies that the degree of devotion is determined by the economic condition of the devotees.

Finally, we discuss the visit efficiency of the pilgrims. The data on the visit efficiency of the pilgrims along with their level of income represent that the middle income earning pilgrims have greater efficiency of visit. Like the degree of devotion, the efficiency to visit to Tarakeswar by the pilgrims is guided by the economic condition of those pilgrims. It implies that greater visit efficiency gradually reduces for the lower income groups and roughly increases for the higher income groups.

The investigation on socio-economic structure of priests exhibits that all priests are educated by the percentage number of priests with secondary and graduation level of education. That is the level of education of priests at Tarakeswar. Similarly, the levels of per capita income of priests are fairly good. Since most of the priests are lying in the high income groups, the data from experience index reflect that most of the sample priests have greater experience about their priesthood profession. Their families are related with this profession from three or four generations. The information about family dependency ratio illuminates that maximum families of sample priests having greater dependency (i.e., 60 per cent to 70 per cent). It implies that the members of priests' families are not so much related with the other productive activities. Most of the families are dependent on only the profession of priesthood to maintain the subsistence of living.

Now, we make different conclusions from different bi-variate data of socio-economic factors. Data about the educational structure along with the level of per capita income indicate that the level of education under all economic categories is quite better. Under lower income groups, the greater percentages of priest have secondary or less level of education. On the other hand, under higher income groups, the percentage numbers of priests have higher level of education. So, the income from this profession is guided by the level of education of priests. The information about the average experience index along with the level of income reflects that the priests from lower income groups having greater experience and higher income groups having lower experience level. It implies that due to greater attachment with the education and other sources of income, the experience is gained by the higher educated priests. We also get the expected results of the calculation of family dependency ratio of priests. That is, the lower income groups have lower family dependency with greater amount and it gradually reduces with the increase in income. On the contrary, the higher income groups having greater family dependency ratio with greater amount, but it reduces with the fall in income. It implies that as the dependency ratio increases then the level of income of that priest also increases that follows the Chayanov Thesis.

Finally, from the discussion about the socio-economic profile of local hospitality providers, we can conclude that maximum providers have secondary level of education. From the earning structure most of the providers earn better level of income to maintain their livelihood, i.e., maximum number of providers earn Rs 700 to Rs 1,000 level of per capita income. Like the priests, the provider groups have also greater experience in their profession. Since they earn a good level of income from their profession, they are engaged with these activities for a long time. Also, the family dependency ratio is higher for providers' group, similar with the priests.

Now, from the examination of educational structure along with the level of income, we get under every educational category the maximum providers having average middle income. On the other hand, lower income groups of providers have lower level of education and the higher income groups having good average level of income. So, the greater level of education helps earn greater income. Now, considering experience index along with level of education of providers, we get the opposite results like the priests, i.e., higher educated groups having greater experience compared to other educated groups. Moreover, the percentage number of providers with higher level of education having greater experience index, gradually reduces. It implies that people wanted to deviate from this profession to other profession, due to greater competition. Furthermore, lower educated groups having the tendency to come to this profession due to the easiest source of income. We get approximately similar results with the priests, where we examine the dependency ratio along with the level of income. The discussion indicates that lower income groups have greater amount of lower dependency ratio. Although, the greater amount of dependency is born by the higher income groups (i.e., Rs 901-Rs 1,000). So, the figs. also roughly follow the Chayanov Thesis.

Therefore, from the previous discussion on socio-economic profile of pilgrims, ritual and non-ritual associates, we can conclude that Religious Culture at Tarakeswar is highly guided by the socio-economic culture of the devotees and which in turn derives the socio-economic culture of the ritual and non-ritual associates at this sacred centre. They are all interdependent with each other. That is, as a whole, the socio-economic culture at Tarakeswar is determined by the Religious Culture, in fact, the Temple Culture. This is the new paradigm of development economics from non-traditional economic aspects.

6

Estimating the Demand for a Cultural Good: A Study of a Religious Site Using Count Data

6.1 Introduction

Text book economics teaches us that the demand for any commodity is related to the utility that it gives. Cultural goods provide utility that is specific to certain cultural milieu. Goods and services that may appear strange to 'outsiders' have a meaningful existence in the eye of the 'insiders'. They like 'beauty' lies in the eye of the beholder. However, once the cultural sphere is defined, the standard law of demand and supply operates. This is what observed by Adam Smith in his discussions on religion in the *Wealth of Nations*.

In this chapter, we are concerned with the demand for a specific cultural good—the demand for pilgrimage activities at Tarakeswar, a religious site of West Bengal. The demand is highly culture specific; it is valuable only to those who are devotionally attached to such practices. However, given this affinity, the demand-supply mechanism operates as in ordinary economics.

This chapter is divided into five sections. The rationale of our study is given in Section 2. Section 3 provides our basic methodologies together with some theoretical underpinning. Section 4 is also divided into four sub-sections. Section 4.1

discusses the procedure by which we collected the data from sample survey. Section 4.2 focusses the analysis of these data used in the study. Section 4.3 gives the econometric results of Count Regression Analysis of the model, and Section 4.4 illuminates a simple simulation study of the data. In Section 5, we conclude the study. In the final section, we give an appendix representing 'Descriptive Statistical Values of Social, Economic and Positional Variables'.

6.2 Rationale of the Study

From the ancient times, temple is the symbol of deity for a Hindu[1]. Tarakeswar is a famous place of Hindu pilgrimage, mainly due to the temple patronage of *'Taraknath'*—the incarnation of *'Lord Shiva'*[2]. Large number of people come to this place from far and near to fulfill their religious requirements. In this study, we try to estimate the socio-economic background of the pilgrims. We also try to find out the factors that explain the pilgrims' decision to visit this sacred place. Pilgrims have varying tendencies to visit this sacred place. However, we can quantify it in terms of the 'religious valuation' of the place. $U = U(d)$

In order to build up the model, we first assume an individual pilgrim's utility function defined over the site. In order to quantify the matter, we assume that a visit to the site is essential for acquiring the holy boon of the site. Thus the utility of a site is directly related to the visit. Total utility is directly proportional to the visit. However, all visits are not equivalent. There are visits on auspicious and non-auspicious occasions. Thus, the pilgrim's choice is not only between visiting the site and not visiting, but also between the appropriate *qualities* of visit[3]. We tend to simplify our analysis by arguing that the *quality* is adequately represented by dates[4] (d), where d is indexed by a finite discrete series $d = \{1, 2, 3, \ldots, D\}$, where D is any positive integer.

...(1)

where d is the date of visit and n is the number of such visits.

We assume that

$$\frac{\partial U}{\partial d} > 0,\ \frac{\partial^2 U}{\partial d^2} < 0.\ U \text{ is a concave function of } d.$$

A pilgrim maximises the utility function subject to some constraints. The first is a budget constraint entailing costs that are borne by the pilgrim. One of the costs is economic—the travelling and other costs associated with the pilgrimage. Another is the hazard risks associated with the journey. Such hazard risks include various aspects such as accident proneness, health hazard and security of the women and children. In most of the pilgrimage centres, there is a huge conglomeration of people within a small space. This accentuates the problem. We assume a risk premium that has to be borne by the pilgrim if he is willing to undertake this activity at a particular date. The budget constraint may be defined as:

$$M = C(d) + r \Pr ob(risk|d) \quad \text{...(2)}$$

where M is the pilgrim's total budget, $C(d)$ is the cost of visit at the date d. Maximisation of (1) with respect to (2) would give:

$$\frac{\partial U}{\partial d} = MEC(d) + MRC(d) \quad \text{...(3)}$$

where *MEC* is the Marginal Economic Cost and *MRC* is the marginal cost of risk –both evaluated at date d. Obviously, the decision to visit at date d will depend on the factors that influence both *MEC* and *MRC*.

Quantifying pilgrim's valuation of a religious site is a contentious issue. There are several attempts at quantifying this seemingly mysterious phenomenon. Without going into such controversy, we have attempted to correlate this unobserved variable with the number of visits of the pilgrim (prior to the present visit) to the site. In Hindu scriptures, repeated visits to a holy place add to the divine virtues. This is particularly true for an easily accessible site like Tarakeswar. Undoubtedly, this approach is not without its frailties. However, it is less subjective than the alternative approaches (such as contingent valuation) and hence free of measurement error.

Thus, in our econometric analysis, we have assumed that:

$$\frac{\partial U}{\partial d} = \varphi(n) \Rightarrow n = \varphi^{-1}(\frac{\partial U}{\partial d}) \qquad ...(4)$$

where n is the number of visits.

6.3 Methodology

We now relate this indirect measure of pilgrim's valuation of a site to a number of socio-economic variables. The most common approach is to use 'Ordinary Least Square Regression' (OLS) with the number of visits of pilgrims as response variable and various socio-economic factors as predictors. But given the discrete and non-negative nature of our dependent variable, the OLS Model is clearly inappropriate as it specifies a conditional mean function $x_i\,\beta$ that may take negative that is the predicted value of y_i is negative and a homoscedastic variance function. With the count data, it is better to the model $E(y/x)$ directly and to choose functional forms that ensure positivity for any value of x_i and any parametric values. When y_i has no upper bound, the most popular of these is the exponential function $E(y/x) = exp\,(x_i, \beta)$. Now if the conditional mean function is, in fact, $exp\,(x_i, \beta)$, the OLS estimator is not consistent for β and the calculated OLS output gives the wrong asymptotic variance matrix. In this case the appropriate models are the Count Data Model.

Count models are employed when y_i takes integer values that represent the number of events that occur. In our study, we estimate several regression models with count data. In addition to the standard Poisson and Negative Binomial Maximum Likelihood (ML) specifications, we provide a number of Quasi-Maximum Likelihood (QML) estimators for count data, like Poisson, Exponential count, Normal count.

Poisson Count Model

The basic Poisson regression model assumes that y_i given $x \equiv (x_1, x_2, x_3 \ldots x_k)$ has a Poisson distribution as in EI Sayyad (1993) and Maddala (1983, section 2.15). The density of y_i given

x under Poisson assumption is completely determined by the conditional mean,

$$m\ (x_i, \beta) = E\ (y_i / x_i, \beta) = exp(x_i, \beta)$$

For the Poisson model the conditional density of y_i given x_i is,

$$prob(y_i / x_{i,}\beta) = \frac{e^{-m(x_{i,}\beta)} m(x_{i,}\beta)^{y_i}}{y!} \text{ for } y = 0,1,2,\ldots\ldots$$

Given a parametric model for $m(x)$ [such as $m(x) = exp\ (x_i, \beta)$ and a random $\{(x_i, y_i), i = 1,2, 3,\ldots N\}$ on (x_i, y_i), it is fairly straightforward to obtain the conditional MLES of the parameters.

The maximum likelihood estimator (MLE) of the parameter β is obtained by maximising the log likelihood function:

$$l(\beta) = \sum_{i=1}^{N} y_i \log m(x_{i,}\beta) - m(x_{i,}\beta) - \log(y_i!)$$

Provided the conditional mean function is correctly specified and the conditional distribution of y is Poisson, the MLE $\hat{\beta}$ is consistent, efficient and asymptotically normally distributed with variance matrix consistently estimated by:

$$\mathrm{v} = var\ (\hat{\beta}) = (\sum_{i=1}^{N} \ (\frac{\partial \hat{m}_i}{\partial \beta} \frac{\partial \hat{m}_i}{\partial \beta}) / \hat{m}_i)^{-1} ; \text{ where } \hat{m}_i = m\ (\mathrm{x_i}, \hat{\beta})$$

But the Poisson distribution imposes important restriction is the equality of the conditional mean and variance.

$$(x_i, \beta)\ var\ (y_i / x_i, \beta) = E\ (y_i / x_i, \beta) = m\ (x_i, \beta)$$

If the mean-variance equality doesn't hold then this model is miss-specified. That's why we provide a number of other estimators for count data, which relax this restriction.

Negative Binomial (ML) Count Model

For the count data, when the variance usually exceeds the mean is called 'the feature of over-dispersion'. The negative binomial distribution has been suggested by some as an alternative to the Poisson, when there is evidence of over-dispersion (Paternoster and Brame, 1997, Osgood, 2000).

The negative binomial model can be estimated by maximum likelihood without much difficulty. The log likelihood for the negative binomial distribution is given by,

$$l(\beta,m)=$$

$$\sum y_i \log(\eta^2 m(x_{i,}\beta)) - (y_i + \frac{1}{\eta^2})\log(1+\eta^2 m(x_{i,}\beta)) + \log\Gamma(y_i + \frac{1}{\eta^2}) - (\log y_i!)$$

$$-\log\Gamma(\frac{1}{\eta^2})$$

where, η^2 is a variance parameter to be jointly estimated with the conditional mean parameter β. the moment conditions under this model are,

$$E\ (y_i / x_i, \beta) = m\ (x_i, \beta)$$

$$var\ (y_i / x_i, \beta) = m\ (x_i, \beta)\ (1+$$

Consistency and efficiency of the negative binomial ML requires that the conditional distribution of y be negative binomial.

Quasi-maximum Likelihood (QML) Method

The QML estimators are robust in the sense that they produce consistent estimates of the parameters of a correctly specified conditional mean, even if the distribution is incorrectly specified. For QML count models, all that is required for consistency is a correct specification of the conditional mean $m\ (x_i, \beta)$.

Exponential Regression Model

Like the Poisson regression model, we specify a conditional mean function $m\ (x_i, \beta)$. The log likelihood function for the exponential distribution is given by

$$l(\beta) = \sum_{i=1}^{N} -\log m(x_{i,}\beta) - {y_i}/{(m(x_{i,}\beta))}$$

The QMLE is consistent even if the conditional distribution

of y_i is not exponential, provided that m_i, is correctly specified.

Normal Count Model

The log likelihood function for the normal distribution is

$$l(\beta)=\sum_{i=1}^{N}-\frac{1}{2}(\frac{y_i-m(x_{i,}\beta)}{\sigma})^2-\frac{1}{2}\log(\sigma^2)-\frac{1}{2}\log(2\pi)$$

Maximising the normal log likelihood function for fixed are correctly specified m_i, provides consistent estimates, even if the distribution is not normal. In our study, we set =1 and robust QML standard errors, when estimating this specification.

For the selection of the best model, we use different information criterions like AIC, SC and HQ:

$$\text{AIC} = -2(\frac{l}{T})+2(\frac{k}{T})$$

$$\text{SC} = -2(\frac{l}{T})+(\frac{k\log(T)}{T})$$

$$\text{HQ} = -2(\frac{l}{T})+ {2k\log(\log(T))}/{T}$$

be the value of the log of the likelihood function with the k parameters estimated using T observations. The model with lowest AIC, BC and HQ is preferred. In our study, negative binomial model is appropriate rather than other models.

6.4 Empirical Results

6.4.1 Sample Data Collection

Over the years, many devotees come to this sacred centre Tarakeswar in order to fulfill their religious requirements. For this purpose, they spend both time and a substantial amount of money at this place. Their spending in turn generates income at this religious centre. Therefore, religion-related activities generate alternative employment opportunities to many people inside and outside of this religious place. Here, we try to estimate the effect of religiosity on some socio-economic features of the pilgrims and also the socio-economic interaction with this sacred place.

Our empirical analysis is based on a broad cross-sectional data set generated for this purpose. A field survey was conducted in the year 2007-2008 to collect the relevant information regarding the socio-economic behaviour of pilgrims coming to Tarakeswar. The survey area was restricted within Tarakeswar municipality area and its surrounding areas of the block of Tarakeswar in West Bengal. A random sample technique was used for collection of data from both male and female respondents, who visited Tarakeswar for religious purpose belonging to various income and occupational groups with different educational levels.

In order to get appropriate coverage, the field survey was spread over three periods. These are (1) the period of maximum attendance of pilgrims, i.e., on three major auspicious seasons such as, *'Sravani Purnima'* in the month of July-August, *'Chaitra Sankranti'* in the month of March-April and *'Sivaratri'* in the month of February and also every Sunday, Monday and usual holidays, (2) that of minimum attendance usually on non-auspicious seasons, and (3) the period in between above two periods.

The information was collected from 733 sample pilgrims by interview and also by systematic observations of these pilgrims. The information relating to the place of origin, demographic particularities, educational and occupational status, house of the pilgrims, reasons or objectives behind their visits, number of their visits, level of income, amount of expenditure for both religious and non-religious purposes, sources of their expenditure, their visit to other religious or non-religious places, etc. all socio-economic characteristics and also the particulars about their level of satisfaction through the interaction with the local hospitality providers both ritual (like priests, pilgrim guides etc.) and non-ritual (like shopkeepers, restaurant owners, rest-room owners, etc.) on the time of their visits to Tarakeswar was collected from sample pilgrims. They were surveyed through personal questionnaire method by using structured and open-ended questionnaire schedule at railway station, bus stand, different rest houses, etc. at Tarakeswar.

To remove the first misconception, the sample was not collected 'by visiting available persons at various points'. Using secondary information available from various sources, we first tried to unravel the pace and pattern of pilgrim's visit. It is revealed that there are several peak and lean periods in the pilgrims' visits corresponding to the degree of holiness ascribed to the shrine. Also the compositions of pilgrims (i.e., social, economic, position and other features) vary across the different seasons. We also conducted a pilot sample survey to augment the secondary findings. The final data collection was thus carefully planned so as to meet this constraint. Our aim was to make the sample as representative as possible.

Nonetheless, it is true that the study does not include persons who have not visited the site. However, in cultural studies, it is difficult to ascertain such potentialities. It is not certain how a person will be charmed by visiting a cultural site. Similarly, a person not so culturally inclined might have visited the place only on group obligation and/or allegiance may be charmed by the site[5]. Thus, it is, however, not a very uncommon phenomenon in the standard practice of cultural economics to consider only the actual visitors (whether potentially inclined or not) of a cultural site. For example, Alberini and Longo (2006), presented their paper on the travel cost method with contingent behaviour questions to estimate domestic visitors' use values of cultural heritage sites in Armenia. Their investigation also shows the significant use value associated with the study and conservation of the cultural heritage sites, improve the cultural experience as well as tourist services that encourage the higher visitation rates by making it easier for the respondents to reach and spend time at this cultural sites (Alberini and Longo, 2006).We first look at some broad features of this data.

6.4.2 Preliminary Data Analysis

The data used in this book, taken from the field survey at Tarakeswar, is completely primary in nature. The survey covered 733 pilgrims arrived at Tarakeswar to fulfill their religious requirements. The various socio-economic features of these pilgrims and their interaction with the local hospitality providers at this sacred centre, Tarakeswar, were recorded as explanatory variables. Here, we consider four types of categorical variables. These are:

- **Socio-economic Variables** – age, caste, sex, house, education and occupational structure of the pilgrims.
- **Positional Variables** – quality of journey towards Tarakeswar, place of residence of the pilgrims (state, region, urban/rural etc.).
- **Satisfaction Variables** – level of satisfaction from deity and a comparison with any other sacred sites visited by the pilgrim[6].
- **Behavioural Variables** – the quality of local hospitality provided by various agents (like priests, pilgrim guides, ritual and non-ritual shopkeepers, restroom owners, etc.).
- **Cost Variables** – The cost variables are defined below. Actually total cost (TC) incurred by a family may be subdivided into various components: cost of travel to the site (C-TRAVEL), cost incurred on religious activities relevant to the shrine (C-RELG.), cost on non-religious secular activities (food, lodging, etc.) (C-NONRELG.), other costs (tax paid, entrance fee, etc.) (C-OTHER). Also we tried to find out total visit costs including all early visits, if any.
- Per visit cost per visitor [PVCPV] = (Total visit costs by a visitor)/(Total number of visit).
- Cost for deity to total family expenditure (Exponential) = C-RELG./ TC.
- Per capita cost for deity and non-ritual activities, per capita cost for visit.

  (PCC) = TC / (Total family member).
- Per capita cost for deity non-ritual activities (PCD-NR) = (C-RELG.+CNONRELG.) / (Total family member visiting the site).

In order to remove the problem of multi-collinearity and other statistical problems, we use the 'Stepwise Regression' among above variables to select an appropriate subset of variables that is strongly related with our dependent variable. Stepwise Regression is one of several computer-based iterative variable-selection procedures which are used to test the effects of a set of independent (predictor) variables on a single dependent (criterion) variable.

In statistics, Stepwise Regression includes regression models in which the choice of predictive variables is carried out by an automatic procedure. Usually, this takes the form of a sequence of F-tests, but other techniques are possible. At each step, we first determine whether any of the variables (already included in the model) can be removed. If none of the variables can be removed, we determine whether a non-yet-included variable can be added. A variable can be added to the model at a step, removed at a following step. The process will continue until no variables could be added or deleted.

From the Stepwise Regression, we sort out some predictive variables like age, level of satisfaction (divine), cost for deity to total family expenditure (Expenditure to total), PCC, quality of journey and manners of priest, ritual and no-ritual selling shopkeepers and per visit cost per visitor (PVCPV) which have significant effect on the explained variable visits.

For the preliminary analysis of available data on the socio-economic features of the pilgrims, we calculated some descriptive summary statistics for some covariates shown in Tables 40 and 41[7].

Table 40: Socio-economic Features of Pilgrims

Characteristics	*No. of Pilgrims*	*% No. of Pilgrims*	*PVCPV*	*PCC*	*Average No. of Visits*
		Age			
Teenagers	68	9.28	73.25	152.79	2.68
Early-Middle-aged	560	76.40	63.50	168.38	4.31
Late-Middle-aged	98	13.37	54.62	183.23	9.22
Old	7	0.96	41.74	735.95	22.57
		Expenditure			
less than 2,000	135	18.42	53.25	143.64	5
2,001-6,000	419	57.16	67.37	168.71	5
6,001-8,000	115	15.69	63.02	213.43	6
8,001-10,000	45	6.14	47.23	160.09	6
10,001 and above	19	2.59	78.03	222.50	7
Total	**733**	**100**	**63.13**	**238.75**	**5**

Source: Author's survey.

Table 41: Results of Descriptive Statistics

Measures	*Variables*					
	Age	*Expenditure (Rs.)*	*Expen. to total*	*PCC*	*PVCPV*	*Visits*
Mean	*29*	*5406*	*0.12*	*171.97*	*63.13*	*5*
Maximum	65	35000	2	1650	1050	44
Minimum	15	900	0.01	37.5	2.78	1
Std. Dev.	9.18	3715.3	0.14	136.02	78.33	5.2
Skewness	1.05	2.15	8.11	4.08	5.08	3.4

Source: Author's survey.

Table 41 indicates that the average value of some covariates (like Expenditure to total, PVCPV, visits) is lower than the extent of variation of those covariates. That is, it displays the presence of the phenomenon of over-dispersion. Therefore, in this study the problem of over-dispersion exists for some important covariates.

6.4.3 Count Regression Analysis

This study utilises four different count data models—Poisson count, Negative Binomial count, Exponential count and Normal count models. In these models, an iterative estimation procedure was adopted due to the parametric non-linearities of these models. A maximum absolute difference of .00001 of all the coefficients in successive iteration was taken as the rule of convergence. Given this rule, the number of iteration required for convergence is maximum 500 times. Now the estimates, co-efficient and the standard errors of the variables under Poisson, Negative Binomial, Exponential and Normal count models are represented by the Table 42.

Table 42 reveals the presence of the phenomenon of over-dispersion for all the covariates. The variance by mean of the dependent variable is always greater than one. In this case, Negative Binomial Count Model is more appropriate than other models. Moreover, the value of different information criterion

Table 42: Estimates of the Poisson, Negative Binomial, Exponential and Normal Models of Pilgrims' Visit Fluctuations

	Model (1) Poisson			*Model (2) Negative Binomial*			*Model (3) Exponential*			*Model (4) Normal*		
Variable	*Co-efficient*	*Standard Error*	*Z-Statistic*	*Co-efficient*	*Standard Error*	*Z-Statistic*	*Co-efficient*	*Standard Error*	*Z-Statistic*	*Co-efficient*	*Standard Error*	*Z-Statistic*
Age	0.027	0.0015	17.75	0.026	0.002	13.246	0.027	0.002	13.006	0.024	0.003	7.123
Divine	0.116	0.055	2.11	0.073	0.065	1.125	-0.079	0.066	-1.194	0.229	0.250	0.913
Exponential	0.251	0.076	3.294	0.082	0.138	0.592	-0.145	0.147	-0.981	0.237	0.066	3.612
Journey	0.099	0.0144	6.88	0.085	0.018	4.859	0.048	0.017	2.757	0.121	0.026	4.744
Manner of Ritual	0.117	0.016	7.072	0.113	0.020	5.780	0.077	0.016	4.746	0.152	0.041	3.706
Manner of Non-ritual	-0.035	0.019	-1.875	-0.026	0.023	-1.128	-0.008	0.022	-0.351	0.026	0.045	0.579
PCC	0.0009	0.00	13.25	0.002	0.000	11.797	0.003	0.000	7.656	0.001	0.000	4.769
PVCPV	-0.010	0.0005	-20.24	-0.011	0.001	-18.754	-0.007	0.001	-9.863	-0.021	0.003	-7.731

Source: Author's calculation.

like Akaike information, Schwarz and Hannan-Quinn criterion are also least in Negative Binomial Model as compared to other count models. That's why, Negative Binomial Count Model is best fitted for our data. However, the Poisson model has the least value of log likelihood. Also, for the proportion of significant variables, Poisson model dominates others.

The estimated effect of these socio-economic factors illuminates that the frequency of visits is positively influenced by the age of devotees at this sacred complex and the test statistic is statistically significant at both one and five per cent level of significance under all four count regression models. It implies that the scared valuation of the site is greater among the pilgrims with higher age.

Now, from the expenditure side of the pilgrims, we considered three cost factors –Exponential, PCC and PVCPV. The estimated effects of PCC are statistically significant in all the count models at either one or five per cent level of significance or both. In the Exponential model, the effect of Expenditure to total is statistically insignificant at both one and five per cent level of significant, although the effect is significant for other count models. Moreover, another cost factor, PVCPV, is found to be inversely related significantly to the affinity to visit at this sacred complex. The behaviour of the cost items appears to be somewhat strange. In order to understand it, we may note that PCC and Exponential are short-run costs, while PVCPV is a component of long run cost. In the short-run, indulging greater cost may not have a negative effect of the decision to visit the shrine. In fact, if such costs are designated as holy, their importance may rise. In the long-run, however, greater per capita cost is not at all sustainable.

In order to fulfill their religious requirements, the devotees have to interact with the local hospitality providers. They also purchase various types of religious and non-religious articles at this sacred centre. Hence, the behaviour and sincerity of these people are crucial towards attaining satisfaction from the performed religious activities surrounding the scared shrine. For ease of analysis, we segregate these hospitality providers under two categories—ritual and non-ritual. Under ritual hospitality providers, we include the priest and ritual articles selling shopkeepers. It is found that their manners[8] positively related with the number of visits and the statistical results are significant under all four models at both five and one per cent level of significance. It illuminates that the healthy behaviour of these hospitality providers would attract more people to Tarakeswar which in turn increase the economic importance of this sacred place. But the non-ritual hospitality providers have no effect in all the models. The result implies the importance of religious commodity providers in the place of pilgrimage.

Another interesting factor is the quality of journey to this sacred centre. All the count regression models represent that the number of visits would increase with improvement of communication towards Tarakeswar and the estimated results are statistically significant at both one and five per cent level of significance. So, better quality of roadways transport and railways transport will attract more pilgrims to this religious place which in turn generate greater economic activities at this sacred centre.

Finally, the survey indicates that the affinity to visit this sacred site is guided by their level of ritual satisfaction from their deity[9]. The greater fulfillment of the pilgrims' religious requirements and proper ritual activities to provide more satisfaction to the pilgrims will attract more of them at this sacred centre. This is shown in the statistically significant result of divine in the Table 42.

6.4.4 A Simple Simulation Study

We, however, try to understand the interaction between the local hospitality providers and the devotees through a simple simulation study. The technique we use is the familiar criterion of stochastic dominance, only applied in directional income movement in the work of Fields, Leary and OK (1998, 1999). In our analysis, we first take any specific count model. We then determine the number of expected visits for each pilgrim under different situations. In each situation, we assume that one of the relevant factors is missing and then calculate the expected number of visits. Thus, each simulation gives us the pilgrim's valuation of Tarakeswar (under the specific count model) when one of the effects is missing. A comparison of this value with the expected value (when no effect is missing) is an indirect indication of the *marginal contribution*[10] of the factor in enhancing the attractiveness of the shrine towards the pilgrim.

A cumulative frequency curve is drawn in each case under different count models. We may call these curves as *marginal curves*. Comparison of these curves based on the idea of stochastic dominance helps us sort out the *marginal effect* discussed above. One distributional change in expected visit is said to stochastically dominate another if percentage of the visits below the given level of visits are smaller in every models with the change in the ranges of actual visit changes. Graphically, this means that a better distribution is one that lies everywhere below or to the right of another.

We have considered four interacting factors—journeys, ritual non-ritual and quality of religious service (priest). It is obvious that the actual visits stochastically dominate the expected visits for all the count models.

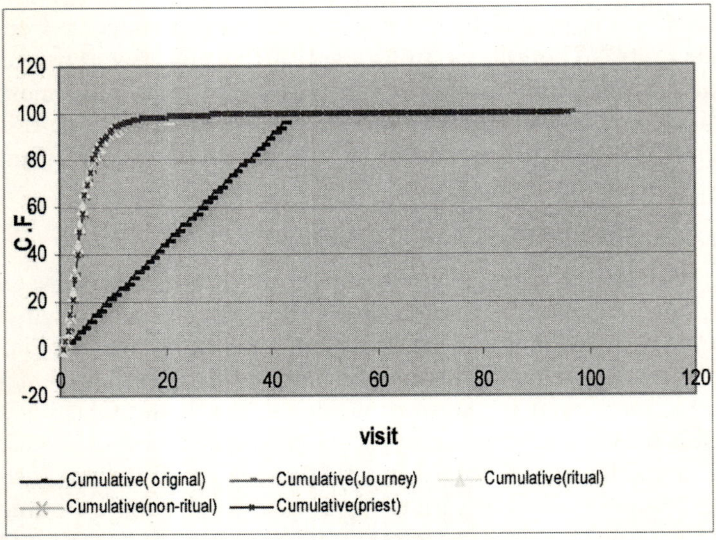

Fig. 29. C.F. of Expected Visit (Poisson Model).

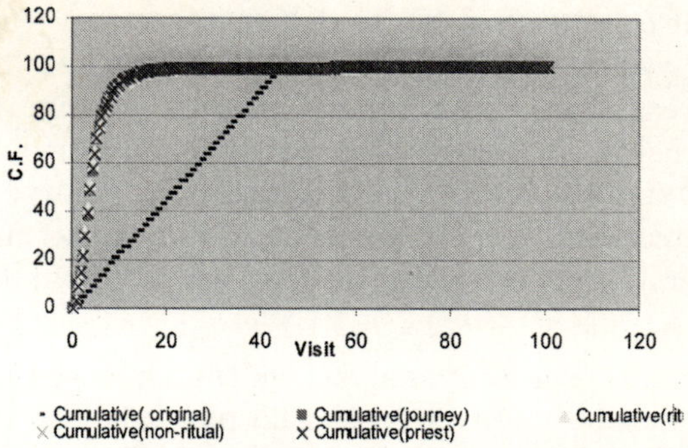

Fig. 30. C.F. of Expected Visit (Negative Binomial Model).

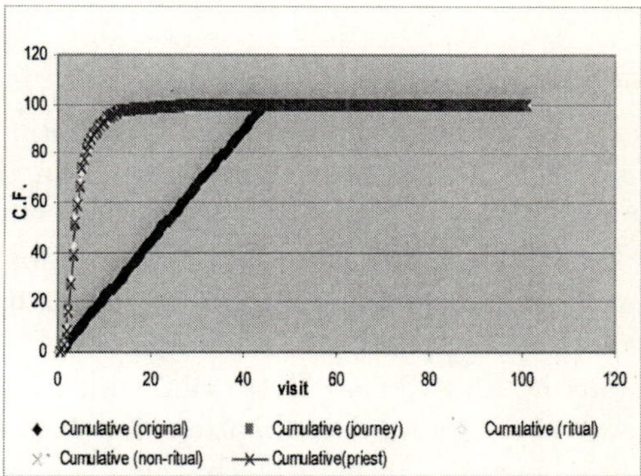

Fig. 31. C.F. of Expected Visit (Exponential Model).

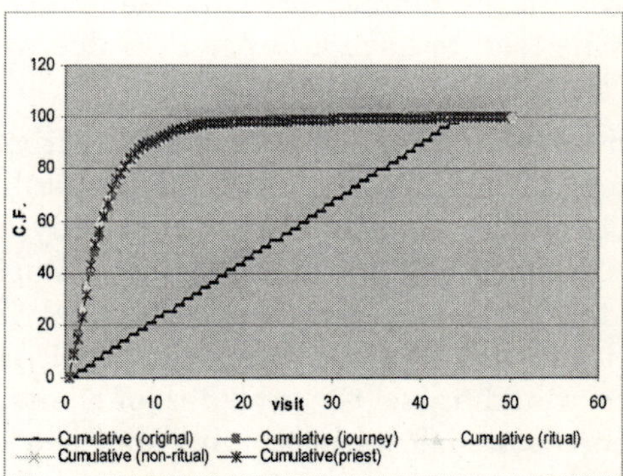

Fig. 32. C.F. of Expected Visit (Normal Model).

The above figs. depict the distribution of changes in visits under four count regression models against the various ranges of visits, respectively. Two things directly follow from these four figures. First, the *marginal effect* is positive for all the factors considered. This is because the cumulative curve sans the factor is stochastically dominated by the curve when the factor is included. Second, however, the marginal curves cross each other thereby showing no first order dominance among the factors.

Therefore, from this analysis we can show the importance of interaction between visits by the pilgrims and the several socio-economic factors at this sacred site. Better behaviour of these groups as well as improved transport and communication facilities will attract more pilgrims to Tarakeswar.

6.5 Conclusion

In this study, we have examined the fluctuation of religious affinity (visits) of the pilgrims depending upon their various socio-economic features and the interaction with the local hospitality providers. Here, we quantify the economic value of this religious centre by the affinity of visits to this sacred centre. Propensity to spend for the deity by per visitor at per their visit may be an internal factor determined by individual psyche. However, its actual realisation depends on a host of socio-economic factors. It is this that brings in within the purview of economics of religion. Our study reveals varying PVCPV for different social groups that are not always concomitant with the number of visits. Generally, people with greater income tend to have a larger PCC due to their higher propensity to spend for the deity.

Another important finding is brought out from an analysis that manners of ritual and non-ritual hospitality providers would affect the frequency of visit significantly. Since, in the absence of any one of the providers, the percentage of expected visits would fall from the percentage of actual visits. So, the betterment of the services provided by inhabitants at Tarakeswar would raise the number of visits, which will generate more economic activities and improve the economic condition of that sacred place.

Thus, we find that a condensed economic cluster is formed surrounding this sacred site and economics of pilgrimage activities is affected by a number of socio-economic factors. The so-called 'spiritual urge' to visit a pilgrimage site is rationalised within a set of quantifiable parameters. It means that if steps are taken to lower the cost of visits, the urban centre of Tarakeswar may gain in respect of popularity and attractiveness. This will help develop the spot further.

Notes

1. Historically temples in India could be traced down to the Gupta Age (in the fourth century AD).
2. In fact, *Lord Shiva* is an ancient deity of India. Archeologists found seals depicting *Lord Shiva* from the ruined cities of the pre-historic Indus valley civilisation-the earliest known human civilisation in India about 5000 BC.
3. There are many aspects in this quality parameter. One important aspect is the time of visit. However, there are other aspects, too. In Hindu pilgrimage traversing, a certain distance by foot may be preferred to any other easy modes of travelling.
4. Here, date does not mean a particular day but a range of dates when the visit is deemed to be most auspicious. For our site Tarakeswar, there are three auspicious dates-belonging to three Bengali months. Out of that one is most dominating.
5. In fact, in our study also many visitors opined that their initial intention for visit was not religious.
6. The satisfaction parameter is indexed by a binary variable.
7. Many of the socio-economic variables were to be excluded due to the strong collinearity with some of the remaining explanatory variables. However, we provide the relevant descriptive information on these variables in the appendix.
8. This psychological factor is captured by a quality variable that captures pilgrim's assessment of their behaviour.
9. This is clearly differentiated from the behaviour of the

ritual providers. A ritual provider may be personally rude though he carries out the ritual activities very sincerely. On the contrary, a good mannered ritual provider may be lacking in sincerity-either due to lack of experience or lack of traditional knowledge about the ritual activities.

10. It is true that positive marginal effect can be found from the estimates themselves. However, the degree of stochastic dominance is not cleared from the regression estimates themselves. For this, we require the simulation study. The curves cross each other failing to show any positive order stochastic dominance.

APPENDIX

Descriptive Statistics of Social, Economic and Positional Variables

Characteristics	*Number of Visits*			
Caste	*Maximum*	*Minimum*	*Average*	*Co-efficient of Variation*
General	44	1	5	109.34
Scheduled Caste	36	1	5	92.43
Scheduled Tribe	13	1	4	106.10
Occupation				
Government	42	1	7	108.58
Other than Government	44	1	5	102.02
Non-worker	23	1	4	95.83
Sector of Origin				
Rural	44	1	5	115.56
Urban	44	1	5	95.48
Area of Origin				
Within West Bengal	44	1	5	103.51
Outside West Bengal	32	1	6	110.95
Sex				
Male	44	1	5	104.54
Female	23	1	5	101.58
Expenditure (in Rs)				
Less than 2,000	32	1	5	100.33
2,001 – 6,000	44	1	5	104.86
6,001 – 8,000	44	1	6	113.60
8,001 – 10,000	18	1	6	68.71
10,000 and above	30	1	7	107.48
Income (in Rs)				
Less than 2,000	20	1	5	88.58
2,001 – 6,000	44	1	5	108.37
6,001 – 8,000	44	1	5	115.49
8,001 – 10,000	42	1	5	103.21
10,000 and above	30	1	6	88.89

7

Unskilled Workers in the Cultural Market: A Case Study of the Utility Providers at a Religious Site

7.1 Introduction

In the modern parlance, livelihood has been defined in a number of ways. However essentially, it measures the income flow and the resilience of the income earner under adversity. In the modern world, livelihood is generated of a wide spectrum of sources—some outside the well-defined arena of main stream economics. Often, cultural activities generate livelihood opportunity for a number of semi-skilled and un-skilled workers related to it. Here, the culture plays a pivotal role in creating an income earning spaces for those who would have otherwise find it difficult to ensure it.

In many sacred centres, people acquire religion in the same way that they acquire other objects of choice and they also evaluate its costs and benefits and acts so as to optimise their utility. It determines the content of religious commodities and the structure, where religion is unregulated and, as a result, a competition among religious firms is pronounced. Along with here considerable portions of the people inside or outside of this centre earn their livelihood by providing different types of secular and non-secular services to them.

Through the discussion of economic behaviour, religious culture is classified from two different aspects—demand side and supply side of this particular culture[1]. From demand side, this culture is consumed by the devotees who arrive to this place to fulfill their religious requirements and also the mental and virtuous pleasure. On the contrary, from the supply side, these demands are fulfilled by the various types of beneficiary groups which are classified into two categories—the group of sacred associates like priests, pilgrim guides and the group of secular associates like rest house owners, shopkeepers, restaurant owners, florists, potters, etc.

In our study, we have selected Tarakeswar, a Hindu pilgrimage site in West Bengal, an Indian state, for analysing the socio-economic pattern and nature of local hospitality providers allied with the religious culture. Economic pattern of this sacred centre depends upon the occupational structure, standard of living of the inhabitants of the town, social-economic infra-structural conditions, etc. The occupational profile reflects that, at Tarakeswer too, a substantial portion of population earns their livelihood from the temple as well as from pilgrims and also the nature and extent of dependency vary from one group to another group.

This chapter is divided into six sections. In the introductory section, we discuss how the cultural activities generate the livelihood opportunities through demand and supply interaction of semi-skilled and unskilled workers in a urban unit. In the second chapter, we illustrate the role of religion in advancing the cultural pace for Tarakeswar. The sample data collection from both secular and sacred hospitality providers are discussed in section 1.3. The identification of various types of information is demonstrated in primary data analysis in section 1.4. Various data analysis on the information and the corresponding results are discussed in section 1.5. This section is also divided into several subsections where we illustrated various types of statistical techniques to examine the above information collected from both secular and sacred hospitality providers. Finally, the conclusion of this chapter is given in the section 1.6.

7.2 Unskilled Workers in the Cultural Space of Tarakeswar

In many sacred centres, religion plays a modern and historic role in advancing or impeding economic development, social progress, moral prosperity, scientific and technological advances and so forth. At Tarakeswar, many sacred and secular groups maintain their livelihood by providing various types of goods and services to the devotees. The greater congregation of pilgrims at this sacred centre would raise the materialistic wellbeing of the people, which in turn accelerate the economic development of this holy place. Therefore, religion has a significant role in fostering the cultural space for Tarakeswar.

We can divide the local hospitality providers into two groups: (1) Sacred (2) Secular. Under the sacred category, the people are doing various ritual roles and functions to facilitate devotees in order to fulfill their religious requirements at Tarakeswar. Under sacred group, there are two types of employees. These are permanent employees, who are appointed by the Temple Estate Authority permanently, and the other is temporary employees, who provide the different ritual services willingly, i.e., for their self-intension and are not appointed by the Temple Estate Authority. At Tarakeswar, the permanent employees are *Mohanta*, head of the monastery of *'Baba Taraknath'* and Chief Priest. Alternatively, private priests and pilgrim guides fall in the temporary employee group. The permanent employees get a fixed income from the government; whereas temporary employees are self-employed.

At Tarakeswar, approximately 86 priests among 109 private priests are actively engaged with the priesthood and rests occasionally provide their services for these ritual activities. Priests come to this pilgrimage centre from various neighbouring districts like Burdwan, Bankurah, Howrah, etc., adjoining blocks like Haripal, Champadanga, etc. and a few come from Bangladesh for the last six to seven generations. Now, another group of religious agents is that of pilgrim guides. They act as an intermediary between pilgrims and priests. They wait for hunting the pilgrims at railway station, bus stand, on the main road leading to the temple. There are 280 registered pilgrim guides and many unregistered pilgrim guides, who maintain their livelihood by assigning in the worships and rites of devotees at the sacred centre of Tarakeswar. The pilgrim guides not only come from local areas at Tarakeswar, but also hail from neighbouring villages and blocks. They earn a respectful amount of income from this profession and also extract money from various ritual and non-ritual functionaries like priests, florists, rest house owners, restaurant owners, and so on contractual basis. They are dependent economically on this sacred centre much more than the priests, because they have no alternative sources of family income, except pilgrim hunting.

Under secular group, there are more or less 60 rest houses (including hotels and *'dharmashalas'*) at Tarakeswar. Most of the rest houses are situated surrounding the temple under the municipal area. Furthermore, many *'yatrinibas'* (rest house) have their own shops to sell the ritual articles like *'batasa'* (sweets), *'nakuldana'* (sweets), *'dala'* (a small basket made by clay containing offering to the deity), *'taga'* (an armlet), etc. to the pilgrims, who come and stay in these *'yatrinibas'* to mitigate their religious needs. By selling those ritual articles, the rest house owners earn a moderate income. The cult of *'Baba Taraknath'* helped develop a number of traders like ritual and non-ritual article selling shopkeepers, restaurants in the neighbourhood of the temple. Approximately 20 fruits selling shops, 32 stationary shops, 60 shops of photographs, toys, images of different gods, 24 shops of fruit pickles and 42 restaurants are situated in the adjoining wards of the temple. They all derive a steady income from their respective professions.

People living far away from Tarakeswar also derive economic benefits directly or indirectly from this religious establishment. There are many stalls in Sheraphuli, Baidyabati, Barakpur region, which sell the religious articles to both Tarakeswar-bound pilgrims as well as resident people. Compared to other stall owners, the stalls near the *Nimai Tirtha Ghat* earn a fairly high and steady income due to the vintage location of their shops and larger inflow of pilgrims to the sacred *ghat* (bank of river Ganga). In this way, the permanent and seasonal traders near and far away from Tarakeswar maintain their livelihood from the patronage of the temple of *'Baba Taraknath'*.

Specially, in different festive seasons like *'Sravani Purnima'*, *'Chaitra Sankranti'*, *'Sivaratri'* and usual holidays, the greater congregation of pilgrims would raise their income manifold. Hence, by facilitating the ritual performances at Tarakeswar to the devotees, the religious agents (i.e., both sacred and secular group) earn their subsistence to maintain their livelihood.

Therefore, livelihoods of a large number of semi-skilled and un-skilled people are closely related to activities generated out of the religious chamber. Many are indirectly dependent on it. Sometimes this importance is so overwhelming that a network of economic activities quite unrelated to the original religious impulse may merge.

7.3 Sample Data Collection

Over the years, many devotees come to the sacred centre of Tarakeswar in order to fulfill their pious interests who spend a substantial amount of money at this place. Their spending in turn generates income at this religious centre. Therefore, religious related activities generate alternative employment opportunities to many people inside and outside of this religious place. Here, we try to estimate the effect of religiosity on some socio-economic features of the hospitality providers and also the socio-economic interaction with this sacred place.

Our empirical analysis is based on a broad cross-sectional data set generated for this purpose. A field survey was conducted in the year 2007-2008, to collect the relevant information regarding the socio-economic behaviour of both sacred and secular groups of hospitality providers at Tarakeswar. The survey area was restricted within Tarakeswar municipality area and its surrounding areas of the block of Tarakeswar in West Bengal. A random sample technique was used for collection of data.

The information was collected from 56 samples of sacred combining with private priests and pilgrim guides and 115 samples of secular group of beneficiaries by interview and also by systematic observations of these beneficiaries. The information relating to this demographic particularities, educational status, house, types of shop, time of engagement with this profession, level of income and expenditure of the family, alternative sources of income, etc., all socio-economic characteristics and also the particulars about their level of satisfaction through the interaction with this sacred centre, were collected from sample hospitality providers at Tarakeswar. They were surveyed through personal questionnaire method by using structured and open-ended questionnaire schedule at railway station, bus stand, different rest houses, etc., at Tarakeswar. We first look at some broad features of this data.

7.4 Primary Data Analysis

The data used in this chapter, taken from the field survey at Tarakeswar, is completely primary in nature. The survey occupies 56 samples of sacred group and 115 beneficiaries of secular group at Tarakeswar. The sacred group covers the private priests and pilgrim guides and the secular group consists of rest house owners, shopkeepers, restaurant owners, barbers, florists, water carriers, potters, milkmen, etc. In most of the Hindu sacred places, more or less homogeneous pattern of socio-cultural and professional levels are maintained by both these sacred and secular groups.

In this study, we segregate the data set into two groups. In the first, we consider the sacred group. The data under this group consist of the information collected from both private priests and pilgrim guides. And the second category is the secular group of providers. Now, we split this category into two classes. These are religious allied business and non-religious related business. Under the religious related business, we consider the shops selling ritual articles and ritual sweets like *'batasha'*, *'nakuldana'*, etc., flower shops, *'dashakarma bhandar'* (shops selling items for preparation of worship) and *'yatrinibas'* (halting rooms for the pilgrims and also provide various ritual articles, sweets to these pilgrims for their worship of god *'Baba Taraknath'* who take rest there). On the contrary, under non-ritual related business, we consider the shops selling pickles, sweets, stationary shops, *'monohari'* shops (shops selling photos, stones, image of idols, various symbols of God, etc.), bronze plated utensil selling shops, hotels, restaurants, grocery shops, studios, jewellery shops, medical stores, shoe shops, book stalls, tea stalls, fruit selling shops, tea stalls, etc.

Under sacred category, we collect data from 36 samples of priests and 20 samples of pilgrim guides and under secular group we collect information from 39 samples of religious related and 76 samples of non-religious related beneficiaries at this sacred center. Due to the nearly homogeneous socio-cultural patterns, professional levels are maintained by both priests and pilgrim guides. So, we analyse the data on sacred group on the basis of 56 samples of them together.

The various socio-economic features of sacred and secular groups and also their interaction with the religious culture at this sacred centre of Tarakeswar are examined in separate way. For the sake of simplicity, we consider four types of categorical variables. These are:

- **Socio-economic Variables –** Age, caste, sex, house, family literacy rate (FL), adult literacy rate, occupational structure, previously engaged with other occupation, number of children to total adult in the family (C/W), family member, gender ratio of the beneficiary groups, number of permanent pilgrims (PP).
- **Positional Variables –** Place of residence of the beneficiary group (state, region, urban/rural, etc.).
- **Satisfaction Variables –** Level of satisfaction from earnings by providing services to the pilgrim[2], dependency on temple, livelihood, years of experience from their profession.
- **Income Variables –** Contribution of income from their profession (both sacred as well as secular services) to Family Income (percentage) [CIPFI= Total income from profession in a family/Total family income], Per Capita Income from Profession (PCPI= Total income from profession in a family/Total family member), Per capita family Income (PCFI = Total income of the family/Total family member), Family's saving propensity from income from their profession (%) [$s_{profession}$ = (Priestly income – family consumption) / Income from profession], Family's saving propensity of the beneficiaries (%) [s = (Family

income – family consumption) /Family income], years of profession.

- **Expenditure Variable –** Consumption propensity of the family (percentage) (c), Consumption propensity from income from their profession (percentage) ($c_{profession}$), Per Capita consumption (PCC).

In our analysis, we distinguish between two sources of income—income from sacred or secular services like priesthood, rest house ownership, shop ownership, etc. and other income. If priest income, for example, dominates, then the family will depend heavily on it. However, just the ratio of priestly income to total family income as captured by the variable CIPFI at a cross-sectional level can't capture this dependant. This is so because the family has long experience with priestly income. If the family in its long run finds priestly income to be dominating, it is likely to affect both $c_{profession}$ and $s_{profession}$. However, the cross sectional values of CIPFI give the contribution only at a point of time. It is highly possible that families have experienced a sudden sprout or contractions in priestly income at an observed point. Thus an otherwise priestly income dominated family may show a high CIPFI. However, $c_{profession}$ and $s_{profession}$ are a rational outcome of consumers' utility maximisation procedure involving expected income. As such there are far better estimates of priest dependent as compared to CIPFI.

In order to remove the problem of multi-collinearity and other statistical problems like endoge.niety problem, we use the Stepwise Regression among above variables to select an appropriate subset of variables that are strongly related with our dependent variable. Step-wise Regression is one of several computer-based iterative variable-selection procedures which are used to test the effects of a set of independent (predictor) variables on a single dependent (criterion) variable.

7.5 Data Analysis and Results

We analyse the sample data of both sacred and secular local hospitality providers on the basis of socio-economic features and the economic interactions with the cultural activities at this sacred center Tarakeswar separately.

We first discuss the consumption scenario of the sacred groups in 1.5.1 (a and b). Then, we turn to secular groups in 1.5.2 (a and b). Finally, in section 1.5.3, we discuss their inequality patterns.

7.5.1 (a) Analysis of Sacred Group

The socio-economic characteristics of the sacred group combining private priests and pilgrim guides can be examined by the results of descriptive statistics. In order to eliminate the problems of multi-collinearity and endogeinity, we use Stepwise Regression and sort out some predictive variables like age, house, number of permanent pilgrims (PP), number of family members, literacy rate, years of experience in their profession (TE), livelihood, consumption as per income from their profession ($c_{profession}$), per capita income from profession (CIPFI). Here house and livelihood are treated as dummy variables. The families under sacred group having house give rank one and without house give rank zero. Likewise, the families maintain their livelihood gives one and cannot maintain livelihood gives zero.

Now, the results of descriptive statistics of sacred group are given by the Table 43. The table represents that average number of people under sacred group are aged. Under this category of profession, a large number of aged providers are essential to the devotees due to the greater experience level. This can also be shown by the average years of experience in this sacred profession. The average years of experience are more or less 33 years. Now, the average literacy rate of sacred group is quite better. The average PCC is higher than the CIPFI and also the average of percentage value of $c_{profession}$ is higher than 100 per cent of total family income from their profession. It implies that the consumption level of the people under sacred group is not entirely covered by their income from their profession. So, the livelihood is not quite satisfactory. Most of them of these families under sacred centre fulfill their rest of the consumption by the income from outside their said profession. The table also represents that per capita family income (PCFI) is almost covered by the per capita professional income (PCPI). It also elucidates that most of the people under this sacred group are unskilled or semi-skilled labour, although they are trying to maintain their livelihood by the income earning entirely from their profession.

Table 43: Descriptive Statistics Results of Sacred Group

Variable	*Mean*	*Minimum*	*Maximum*	*Standard Deviation*	*Skewness*
PCC	1015.98	500	1400	260.03	-0.35
Age	50.20	26	76	12.50	0.18
PP	129.64	60	220	50.85	0.52
Family Members	6.29	3	13	2.81	0.95
No. of Literates	5.48	3	10	2.32	0.81
Years of Experience	32.80	10	58	11.49	0.38
$c_{profession}$ (percentage)	110.20	47.15	161.73	24.29	-0.31
PCPI	1009.23	409.09	2827.78	518.50	2.19
CIPFI (percentage)	79.90	41.02	100	21.31	-0.55
PCFI	1376.24	510.42	3500	633.36	1.36

Source: Author's Calculation.

(b) Determinants of Income of the Sacred Group

An economist is interested in studying the factors that may determine the earning potential of an individual or a group. In our analysis, the two important groups of unskilled workers are the sacred and secular groups. In order to formulise the relation, we use PCC as a proxy to income. The factors that determine the income and the productive capacity of the unskilled labourers are many. Broadly, we can speak of the following functional relation:

$$c = c\,(K_f, H_f, S_f) \qquad \text{...(1)}$$ [3]

where, K_f is the stock of physical asset of the family,

H_f is the stock of human capital of the family and

S_f is the other relevant factors.

In our model, we use several parameters to capture these three dimensions that are relevant in the sacred market.

For example, literacy rate acts as a proxy of some human capital parameters of the family. Similarly, house, PP and saving out of the professional income are the three dimensions of physical capital. Among other factors, the total earning members of the family, job satisfaction and income from other sources are proxied by CIPFI. Given the analysis of James and Sharpe, these factors satisfactorily explained the consumption pattern of the pilgrims.

As for the estimable functional form, we use a linear structure, following James and Sharpe. Since the dependent variable is truncated between zero and one, we use the Tobit Regression.[4]

Table 44: Tobit Estimates on Dependent Variable PCC

Determinants	*Coefficient*	*Std. Error*	*z-stat*	*p-value*
Intercept	-26.44	251.79	-0.11	0.92
Age	-16.80	2.26	-7.45	<0.000
House	555.32	54.27	10.23	<0.000
PP	1.55	0.33	4.65	<0.000
Family Members	-180.50	24.50	-7.37	<0.000
No. of Literates	114.28	20.41	5.60	<0.000
Years of Experience	16.80	2.51	6.68	<0.000
Livelihood	-78.21	19.43	-4.03	0.000
Cprofession (Percent)	8.73	1.55	5.61	<0.000
PCPI	0.25	0.05	5.36	<0.000
CIPFI	-0.22	0.89	-0.25	0.802
PCFI	0.01	0.01	0.75	0.451

Log-likelihood	-281.85		Akaike criterion	589.70
Schwarz Criterion	616.03		Hannan-Quinn	599.91
Test statistic: Chi-square(2) = 42.56 with p-value = 0.000				

Source: Author's Calculation.

The results of estimates under this regression are given by the Table 44. This table reveals that the covariates age, number of the family member, livelihood are negatively related with family PCC of religious service providing groups. The estimates of all these covariates are statistically significant at both five per cent as well as one per cent levels of significance, except CIPFI and PCFI. But the variables house, number of permanent pilgrims (PP), year of experience in their profession (TE) and $c_{profession}$ are positively associated with PCC of sacred service providing families and all estimates of these variables are statistically significant at both five per cent as well as one per cent levels of significance. The results explore that as the number of permanent pilgrims increases then the PCC will also increase through increasing per capita income. Similarly, as years of experience in their profession increases then PCC also increases through enhancing the PCPI. So, we can say that the socio-economic characteristics of sacred group are absolutely dominated by the shrine of this sacred center of Tarakeswar.

7.5.2 (a) Analysis of Secular Group

Under secular group, we discuss these features separately for religious related hospitality providers and non-religious related providers. The descriptive statistical results of both the religious related and non-religious related hospitality provider groups are given in the Tables 45 and 46. By comparing these two tables, we can say that the average age of religious related providers is lower than the average age of non-religious related providers. But the average number of child to total adult family members (C/W) is higher for the religious related provider families than the non-religious related provider families and also the average family literacy rate of religious related providers is higher than the average value of non-religious related providers. Although, the years of experience in the profession of non-religious related hospitality providers are higher than the religious related hospitality providers. But the average value of income from the business to total family income (CIPFI) is higher for the religious related goods and service providers than the average value of CIPFI of non-religious related providers. The similar phenomenon is shown in case of per capita family income (PCFI) and per capita family consumption (PCC), for both hospitality provider groups.

It illuminates that the source of earning and the consumption of religious related hospitality providers are largely guided by the divine of this sacred centre of Tarakeswar than the non-religious related hospitality providers. Moreover, the extent of variation among two variables—CIPFI and PCC—elucidates that the standard of living of religious related goods providers is slightly better than the non-religious associated goods providers. The comparison among these tables also represents that PCPI is higher for the religious related service providers than the non-religious related service providers. Therefore, from these statistical results, we can say that the socio-economic features of secular group (mostly religious related service providers) are largely guided by the exaltedness of this holy place.

Table 45: Descriptive Statistical Result of Secular Groups Selling Religious Related Goods and Services

Determinants (religious)	*Measures*				
	Mean	*Minimum*	*Maximum*	*Standard Deviation*	*Skewness*
Age	41.39	22	65	9.63	0.43
Other Earning Members	0.56	0	2	0.61	0.59
Total Family Members	4.64	2	16	2.54	3.06
C/W (percentage)	16.58	0	66.67	18.18	0.81
CIPFI (percentage)	66.17	16.67	100	22.87	-0.45
FL (percentage)	65.52	25	100	20.70	0.08
TE	32.39	10	80.00	16.45	1.10
$c_{profession}$ (percentage)	119.24	66.67	400	67.02	2.80
PCFI	2281.07	972.22	4137.93	583.97	0.53
PCPI	1523.14	465.12	3103.45	668.36	0.33
PCC	1519.52	833.33	2413.79	393.09	0.25

Source: Author's Calculation.

Table 46: Descriptive Statistical Result of Secular Groups Selling Non-religious Related Goods and Services

Determinants (non-religious)	*Measures*				
	Mean	*Mini-mum*	*Maxi-mum*	*Standard Deviation*	*Skewness*
Age	43.18	26	60	9.59	0.11
Other Earning Members	1.04	0	3	0.84	0.62
Total Family Members	5.14	1	18	2.98	2.87
C/W (percentage)	15.87	0	125	21.22	2.13
CIPFI (percentage)	63.65	21.43	100	19.17	0.09
FL (percentage)	63.55	25	100	20.29	0.11
TE	33.99	4	80	14.62	0.71
$C_{profession}$ (percentage)	59.67	20	100	18.81	0.29
PCFI	2237.33	696	4091	823.93	0.29
PCPI	1401.61	483.87	4000	611.94	1.48
PCC	1409.65	521.74	3000	433.52	0.57

Source: Author's Calculation.

Table 47: Comparison between Religious and Non-religious Related Goods and Services Providing Hospitality Providers on the Basis of Some Socio-economic Structures

	Religious		*Non-religious*	
Features	Percentage *of Less than Average*	Percentage *of More than Average*	Percentage *of Less than Average*	Percentage *of More than Average*
Average Literacy Rate	38.89	61.11	47.37	52.63
Average Adult Literacy Rate	58.33	41.67	56.58	43.42
Average PCFI	50	50	47.37	52.63
Average PCC	52.78	47.22	59.21	40.79

Source: Author's Calculation.

The similar result can be obtained from the comparative study on some socio-economic features of both religious related and non-religious related hospitality providers, given in the Table 47. The table explores that under religious related hospitality providers, the literacy rate of 38.89 per cent families of total samples is less than the average literacy rate. This percentage fig. is lower than the percentage number of families (47.37 per cent) under non-religious related hospitality providers. Consequently, under religious related hospitality providers, the percentage number of families with more than average literacy rate is greater than the percentage number of families of non-religious related hospitality providers. It implies that the educational status of religious related secular group is quite better than the non-religious related secular group, although we get opposite result in case of average literacy rate. Now, the percentage number of families under religious related hospitality providers with less than average per capita income is higher than the percentage number of families under non-religious hospitality providers. On the contrary, the percentage number of families under religious related hospitality providers with less than average per capita income is lower than the percentage number of families under non-religious hospitality providers. It represents that the relative poverty level of non-religious allied hospitality providers is slightly greater than religious allied hospitality providers.

(b) Determinants of Income of the Secular Group

The 'Tobit Regression Analysis' is also used to examine the relationship between several independent or predictor variables and a dependent or criterion variable. It treated almost in the same way and that of the sacred group. Here, the determining factors are more or less the same. In our analysis, per capita consumption of the secular hospitality providers is treated as a dependent variable. Here, covariates previously engaged with other activities and categories of business are used as dummy variables. Under religious related hospitality providers, we rank the category of business in the following way – ritual article selling shops rank first, *'yatrinibasas'* rank second, *'dashakarma bhanders'* rank third, ritual flower shops rank fourth. Again under non-religious related hospitality providers, we give rank first for hotel, rank second for *'monohari'* shops, shops of ritual stone and metal products, stationary shops, shops of photos, stone article, shops of bronze plated utensils, etc., rank third for shops of pickles and sweets, rank fourth for shops of shoes, studios, electric shops, tea stalls, jewellry shops, garment shops, book stalls, shops of fertiliser, grocery shops, etc. and rank fifth for fruit shops.

Under the Tobit Regression Analysis, we examine the significant effect of some predictive covariates like family members, family literacy rate, other earning members, $c_{profession}$, CIPFI, PCFI and PCPI on the explained variable PCC. The results of both secular groups can be represented by the Tables 48 and 49, respectively.

Table 48: Estimates of Tobit Regression Analysis of Religious Related Hospitality Providers

Determinants	*Coefficient*	*Std. Error*	*z-stat*	*p-value*
Intercept	-449.22	320.47	-1.40	0.16
Any Other Earning Member	-172.06	84.72	-2.03	0.04
CIPFI	8.44	2.41	3.51	0.00
Category of Dokan	-32.18	58.78	-0.55	0.58
Total Family Members	-8.01	20.91	-0.38	0.70
Family Literacy	1.88	1.51	1.24	0.21
PCFI	0.33	0.08	4.23	0.00
$c_{profession}$ (percentage)	3.89	1.14	3.42	0.00
PCPI	0.16	0.11	1.53	0.13

Log-likelihood	-234.57		Akaike criterion	489.13
Schwarz Criterion	504.97		Hannan-Quinn	494.66
Test statistic: Chi-square(2) = 1.92 with p-value = 0.38				

Source: Author's Calculation.

We get significant results only for four determinants under Tobit Regression of religiously related hospitality providers represented by the Table 48). Here we obtain statistically significant results for CIPFI, any other earning members, PCFI and $c_{profession}$ under this analysis. The factors CIPFI, PCFI and $c_{profession}$ are directly related with PCC and the results are statistically significant at both five per cent as well as one per cent levels of significance. But the covariate the number of any other earning member and category of *dokan* (business) are indirectly related with PCC. Although the estimates of the covariates category of *dokan*, PCPI, total family members and family literacy are not statistically significant. Therefore, this table explores that the PCC of religiously related hospitality providers is steered by the earnings associated with the religiously related cultural activities. Moreover, we can also argue that the PCC at this sacred place is powered by the number of people associated with the religious related services. Therefore the table represents that having significant estimates are guided by the shrine of this holy place, Tarakeswar.

The interactions among socio-economic features of non-religious related hospitality providers are given in the Table 49. The table reveals that the covariates number of earning members and number of family member are negatively related with PCC of the families under non-religious allied secular groups. But all these results are statistically insignificant. We get significant results for $c_{profession}$, CIPFI, PCFI and family literacy rate. The table shows that the estimates of these determinants are statistically significant at both five per cent as well as one per cent levels of significance, except one, i.e., family literacy rate. Like the religious related hospitality providers, we get similar phenomenon for non-religious related hospitality providers from this table. It implies that if the proportions of income from business to total income as well as per capita family income increases then per capita family consumption will also increase.

Therefore, from this analysis, we say that PCC of secular group depends significantly on the earning from their profession, which in turn depends on the cultural activities at this sacred centre. However, rise in earnings of these two

Table 49: Estimates of Tobit Regression Analysis of Non-religious Related Hospitality Providers

Determinants	*Coefficient*	*Std. Error*	*z-stat*	*p-value*
Intercept	-716.39	383.60	-1.87	0.06
Any Other Earning Member	-23.24	49.89	-0.47	0.64
CIPFI	6.89	3.09	2.23	0.03
Category of Dokan	38.45	54.53	0.71	0.48
Family Literacy	2.21	1.28	1.72	0.08
PCFI	0.31	0.06	5.55	<0.00
$c_{profession}$ (percentage)	4.65	0.87	5.38	<0.00
PCPI	0.24	0.07	3.27	0.00
Total Family Members	-13.98	19.53	-0.72	0.47

Mean Dependent Var	1409.65		S.D. dependent var	433.52
Censored Obs	0		sigma	175.30
Log-likelihood	-500.49		Akaike criterion	1020.99
Schwarz Criterion	1044.30		Hannan-Quinn	1030.30
Test statistic: Chi-square(2) = 4.86 with p-value = 0.088				

Source: Author's Calculation.

secular groups will accelerate the economic development through raising the level of consumption at this place. For that reason, the betterment of the services provided by the secular groups would raise the economic importance through increasing the religious attractiveness of this holy place, Tarakeswar.

7.5.3 Measurement of Inequality between both Religious and Non-religious Related Goods Providing Hospitality Providers

Moreover, in order to measure the degree of inequality in the distribution of per capita family income among religious and non-religious related hospitality providers, we use the device, Lorenz Curve. The Lorenz curves of both the secular groups can be shown by the Figures. 33 and 34, respectively. And the results on Gini co-efficient are given in the table 50. The table exhibits that the value of Gini co-efficient of non-religious related hospitality providers is higher than the value of Gini co-efficient of religious related hospitality providers, signifying that the area between egalitarian line and Lorenz curve, i.e., the area of concentration of non-religious associated goods providers is higher than the area of religious associated goods providers. It illuminates that the degree of inequality in income distribution is higher for the non-religious associated secular groups than the religious associated secular groups. These discussions on socio-economic features of both secular groups reveal that socio-economic condition of religious allied secular groups is better than the non-religious allied secular groups at this sacred centre, Tarakeswar.

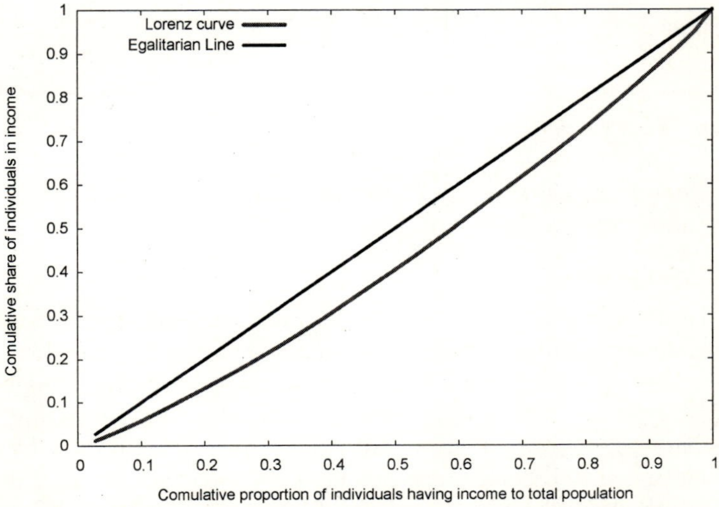

Fig. 33: Lorenz Curve of Religious Related Hospitality Provider.

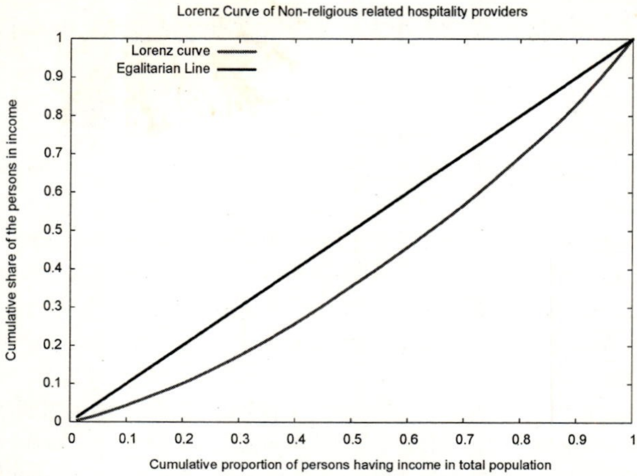

Fig. 34: Lorenz Curve of Non-religious Related Hospitality Provider.

Table 50: Result of Gini Co-efficient

Feature	*Secular Group*	*No. of Observations*	*Gini Co-efficient*	*Estimated Population Value*
CIPFI	Religious Related	36	0.137	0.141
	Non-religious Related	76	0.207	0.210

Source: Author's calculation.

Therefore, we can say that the socio-economic culture is dominated by the Religious Culture at this sacred centre.

7.6 Conclusion

In this study, we discuss about the socio-economic characteristics of both sacred and secular hospitality providers and also we examine the interactions among these characteristics. The study reveals that both the goods and services providing groups maintain their livelihoods by associating with the various religious and non-religious cultural activities. Various statistical results under sacred service providing group explores that under priestly and pilgrim guide profession years of experience is a vital factor. The availability of permanent pilgrims depends upon the years of professional experience of the providers. Besides this, the per capita consumption of sacred group depends upon the per capita income acquired from their profession. So, many unskilled and semi-skilled labourers are engaged with this profession to maintain their livelihood, which is largely guided by the religious importance of this sacred centre.

On the contrary, similar phenomenon is obtained from the analysis of secular hospitality providers. Under this secular group, the economic condition is better for the religious related service providers than the non-religious related providers. And also the degree of inequality in income distribution is lower for the religious allied goods providing families than the non-religious related families. Moreover, the literacy condition is also higher for religious related service providers than the non-religious related service providing group. That is, the socio-economic conditions of the former group are healthier than the latter group. Furthermore, the PCC of non-religious allied hospitality providers directly depends on the income from their corresponding business. Therefore, we conclude that the socio-economic conditions are steered by the Religious Culture, in fact Temple Culture, at this sacred centre, Tarakeswar.

Notes

1. There has been a lot of discussion regarding the relationship between religion and economic decision-making. For example see Iannaconce (1988, 1990, 1991), Deheija and Deheija (1993), Munger (2006), James and Sharpe (2007), Desender, Castro and Escamillade León (2011).
2. The satisfaction parameter is indexed by a Binary variable.
3. The model is a variants James Sharpe Model (2007), where the relationship is drawn for religious affinity and economic parameters.
4. Incidentally this is the form used by James and Sharpe in their formulation.

8

Main Findings and Conclusion

The entire research study on cultural economics especially emphasises on Temple Culture, with reference to a case study of Tarakeswar. It is terminated by giving the conclusion that the socio-economic development of Tarakeswar block as well as municipality is fully dependent upon the Religious Culture of the temple of *'Baba Taraknath'*. The municipal authority, the railway authority and various local hospitality groups at Tarakeswar are socio-economically dependent on the Temple Culture to a great extent. We have summarised the main results in each chapter on the relevant aspects of Temple Culture. This chapter merely places them together to provide an overall summary and conclusion of all these findings.

From the first chapter, we conclude that under human civilisation, man has moved from the personal small group interaction to the large impersonal system. The journey towards a system of impersonal exchange will increase transaction cost and the problem of integrating divert knowledge into socially useful and productive entity. Under this endeavour, religion is substitute of the genetic urge for personal interaction towards a complex society where exchange is largely impersonalised. Along with religion, arises the enormous force for constructing social capital which is very important for economic prosperity in the complex society. That's why, in spite of many costs involved in visiting a sacred site, the devoted persons cannot ignore their visits to these sacred centres.

Here, we also conclude that an association may arise between socio-economic culture and Economic Culture through 'market'. Through generation of multiplier effect and external effect, Religious Culture is related with the Economic Culture, which is known as the study of *'Economics of Religion'*. In this chapter, we represent the mechanism of economics of religion at this sacred centre, Tarakeswar, by the various cultural agents from both demand side and supply side.

We discussed in detail the prevailing mode of thinking in the main stream literature on the role of religious culture and its impact in the mainstream economic activities in the third chapter. It is clear that almost all the thinkers opine the crucial role that religion plays in determining the socio-economic fabric of the society that man has erected. However, we require a rigorous quantitative documentation of these phenomena at a micro-level from an economist's viewpoint. Such analysis would help us juxtapose the broader macro fabric that all the thinkers visualise. Very few studies in this regard are available at hand. These bring out the importance of the present study and its role in a broader fabric.

In order to measure pilgrim's valuation of a site to a number of socio-economic variables, we use the most common approach, Ordinary Least Square Regression (OLS), with the number of visits of pilgrims as response variable and various socio-economic factors as predictors. But given the discrete and non-negative nature of our dependent variables, the OLS model is clearly inappropriate. In this case, the appropriate model is the count data model. In our study, with count data, we estimate several regression models like Poisson, Negative Binomial, Exponential count, and Normal count. Here, we also try to understand the interaction between the local hospitality providers and the devotees through a simple simulation study. The technique we shall use is the familiar criterion of stochastic dominance. Under this study, a cumulative frequency curve is drawn in each case under different count models. Comparison of these curves, based on the idea of stochastic dominance, helps us sort out the *marginal effect* in expected visit. The expected visit is said to stochastically dominate another if percentage of the visits below the given level of visits is smaller in every model with the change in the ranges of actual visit changes. We analyse the socio-economic characteristics of both sacred and secular groups of local hospitality providers by employing the Tobit Regression Analysis and Multiple Regressions Analysis, respectively. In this chapter, we also derive the Lorenze curve and Gini co-efficient to examine the degree of inequality in income distribution among the various religious related and non-religious related hospitality providers.

Therefore, the entire research study can illuminate the degree of association between Religious Culture with the Socio-Economic Culture in this sacred centre, Tarakeswar.

Here, we examine the economics of pilgrimage activities at Tarakeswar. The study exposes that the fluctuation of religious kinship (visits) of the pilgrims depends upon their various socio-economic features and the interaction with the local hospitality providers. By the affinity of visits to this sacred centre, we quantify the economic value of this religious place. From this study, we can say that the actual realisation of their visit depends on the socio-economic factors like cost for deity, per capita consumption, age, satisfaction, etc. and also the manners of ritual and non-ritual hospitality providers. So we conclude that the betterment of the services provided by the ritual and non-ritual hospitality providers at Tarakeswar would raise the number of visits, which in turn generate more economic activities and improve the economic condition of that sacred place. Therefore, we can say that the economic development of this sacred centre is extremely guided the temple culture at Tarakeswar.

Finally, we discussed about the socio-economic characteristics of both sacred and secular hospitality providers at Tarakeswar and also we examine the interactions among these characteristics with their economic activities (like PCC) at this place. The study reveals that both the hospitality providing groups maintain their livelihood by associating with the various religious and non-religious cultural activities. Therefore, from this study, we can conclude that the socio-economic nature and the economic activities are largely dominated by the religious ethnicity at this sacred centre.

Therefore, from the overall study, we can conclude that the socio-economic activities of Tarakeswar as well as its inhabitants are principally steered by the religious activities of the temple of *'Baba Taraknath'*. The healthier services will attract more pilgrims to this place, will generate greater economic activities, and will, in turn, accelerate the economic development of this holy place.

But in recent times, it is seen that the tendency to visit Tarakeswar by the pilgrims gradually reduces due to some reasons. Different political hazards, some administrative inefficiency, infrastructural problems like lack of toilets, bathrooms, waiting rooms, concrete roads, pavements, proper drainage system, etc. are responsible for this pessimistic phenomenon. Some problems are also originated from supply side of cultural agents. Especially in different auspicious seasons like *'Sravani Purnima'*, *'Chaitra Sankranti'* and some usual holidays, some local hospitality provider groups use to deceive many pilgrims for their personal materialistic gains. For that reasons, the devotees are failed to fulfill their worships with full of mental satisfaction. That's why, the desire to visit Tarakeswar by the pilgrims gradually reduces. In order to attract more pilgrims to Tarakeswar, some remedial measures should be taken. Firstly, the above problem should be addressed, i.e., better infrastructural facilities maintaining bio-remediation, greater administrative efficiency drive away various systematic problems and attract more pilgrims to this sacred centre. Further, in the times of micro-level investigation, different cultural agents suggested to set up and improve more recreational components like parks, picnic gardens, boating ponds, etc. to attract not only pilgrims but also many tourists. In this way, Tarakeswar will become a famous sacred tourist centre in West Bengal in Eastern India.

Bibliography

Alberini Anna and Longo Alberto (2006), "Combining the travel cost and contingent behaviour methods to value cultural heritage sites: Evidence from Armenia", Springer Science+Business Media B.V. 2006, *Journal of Cultural Economics.*

Alexis de Tocqueville (1851), *Democracy in America*, Vol. II, New York: A S. Barnes & Co.

Arnold J. Toynbee (1954), *A Study of History*, Vol. VII, Oxford University Press, 1934.

Arrow (1982), 'A Cautious Case for Socialism'. In Howe, (ed.), *Beyond the Welfare State.* New York: Schocken Books.

Baby M.D. (2003), Economics of Sabari Pilgrimage with Special Reference to the Households in Erumely Gram Panchayat, Thiruvananthapuram, *Final Project Report* (Ref. No. 31/99), Supported by Kerala Research Programme on Local Level Development (KRPLLD), Centre for Development Studies, Kerala.

Barro, Robert J. and McCleary, Rachel M. (2003), "Religion and Economic Growth across Countries," *American Sociological Review*, Vol. 68, pp. 760-81.

Bloomfield, P. (1976), *Fourier Analysis of Time Series: An Introduction*, Princeton University, John Wiley and Sons, New York.

Bober, M.M. (1948). *Karl Marx's Interpretation of History.* 2nd (ed.) Harvard Economic Studies. Cambridge: Harvard University Press.

Chakrabarti, Prafulla (1984), *Social Profile of Tarakeswar*, Calcutta, Firma KLM Pvt. Ltd., Kolkata.

Choi Andy S., Papandrea Franco and Bennett Jeff (2007), "Assessing cultural values: developing an attitudinal scale", *Journal of Cultural Economics,* Springer Science+Business Media, LLC 2007.

Chopra, P N. (1982), edited: *Religion and Communities of India*, New Delhi : Vision Books.

Comte August, (1988), *Introduction to Positive Philosophy*, Cambridge, Hackett.

Daniel Pals, *Seven Theories of Religion.*

Das T K. and Datta Roy, (2003), "Market of Religion in West Bengal", *West Bengal Economy – Some Contemporary Issues*, Allied Publications Private Limited, pp. 470-499.

Datt, Ruddar and Sundharam, K.P.M. (2005), *Indian Economy*, S. Chand & Company Ltd.

District Statistical Hand Book, Hooghly, 2003, B.A.E. and S., Government of West Bengal.

Engels Friedrich (1969), *Manifesto of the Communist Party*, Karl Marx, February, 1848; Marx/Engels Selected Works, Vol. 1, Progress Publishers, Moscow, pp. 98-137.

Fishman, G S (1969), *Spectral Methods in Econometrics.* Cambridge: Harvard University Press.

Freeman James M. (1975), Religious Change in a Hindu Pilgrimage Centre: Review of Religious Research, Vol. 16, No. 2, *Comparative and Longitudinal Studies*, pp. 124-133, Published by: Religious Research Association, Inc.

Glaeser, Edward L. and Sacerdote, Bruce (2002), "Education and Religion," Manuscript.

Heineck G. (2006), "The relationship between religion and fertility: Evidence for Austria", *Journal of Population Economics*, 3, University of Erlangen-Nuremberg, Department of Economics, Nuremberg, Lange Gasse 20, 90403, Germany.

Heineck G. (2001), "The Determents of Church Attendance and Religious Human Capital in Germany: Evidence from Panel Data", *Discussion Paper No. 263;, Deutsches Institut für Wirrtschaftsforschung (DIW)*, University of Bamberg, Berlin.

Iannaccone L R. (1988), "Introduction to the Economics of Religion", *Journal of Economics Literature*, Vol. XXXVI (September 1998), pp. 1465-1996.

Iannaccone L R. (1992), "Sacrifice and Stigma: Reducing Free-riding in Cults, Communes and other Collectives", *Journal of Political Economy*, Vol. 100, No. 2, pp. 271-291.

Kevin L. Kliesen and Frank A. Schmid (2004). "Fear of hell might fire up the economy," *The Regional Economist*, Federal Reserve Bank of St. Louis, Issue, July.

Marx Karl. (1844), "A Contribution to the Critique of Hegel's Philosophy of Right", *Deutsch-Französische Jahrbücher*, February.

Montalvo J G and M. Reynal-Querol (2003), "Religious Polarisation and Economic Development", *Economic Letters.*

Mueller C. Dennis (1979), *Public Choice*, Cambridge University Press.

Putnam, R (2000), Bowling Alone: The Collapse and Revival of American Community, *Journal of Democracy,* 6:1, New York, Simon and Schuster.

Robert, H. Nelson (2002), "Religion Economics and Market Paradox": An Interview, an article "Subscribe to Religion and Liberty".

Robert, H. Nelson (2001), *Economic as Religion: From Samuelson to Chicago and Beyond*, University Park: Penn State University Press.

Senapati N. (2002), *Glimpses on the History of Tarakeswar and Foundation of Tarakeswar Temple*, Sree Durga Library, Tarakeswar, India.

Sil, Benimadhav, *Bengali Almanac* (for the year 1408, 1409, 1410, 1411, 1412 and 1413), Akshay Library, Kolkata, West Bengal.

Smith A. (modern version, 1965), *An Inquiry into the Nature and Causes of the Wealth of Nation*, *(1776)*, New York: The Modern Library.

Smith J Z (1982), *Imagining Religion: From Babylon to Jonestown*. Chicago, IL: University of Chicago Pres.

Stein, Burnton, The Economic Function of a Medieval South Indian Temple, *Journal of Asian Studies*, 1960.

Thaper, Romila (1966), *History of India*, Penguin.

Timur, Kuran (2004), *Islam and Mammon: The Economic Predicaments of Islamism,* Princeton: Princeton University Press.

Vidyarthi, L P, Jha, M. and Saraswati, B. N. (1979), *The Sacred Complex of Kashi: A Microcosm of Indian Civilisation*, Delhi, India.

Weber, Max (1958), *The Protestant Ethic and the Spirit of Capitalism*, Charles Scribner's Sons, New York.

Wooldridge J M (2002), *Econometric Analysis of Cross Section and Panel Data*, Cambridge MA, MIT Press.

Further Readings

Armstrong, Karen (1993). *A History of God: The 4000 Years Quest of Judaism, Christianity, and Islam*, New York, A.A. Knopf, p. 460.

Basu Kaushik (1983), On Why We Do Not Try to Walk Off Without Paying After a Taxi Ride, *Economic and Political Weekly*, Vol. 18.

Barth, A. (1963), *Religions of India*, Varanasi, Sanskrit Series Office, XXIV.

Berger, L Peter (1967), *The Sacred Canopy: Elements of a Sociological Theory of Religion*, Garden City. New York, Doubleday.

Berk Richard and MacDonald John (2008), "Overdispersion and Poisson Regression", *Journal of Quantitative Criminology,* Vol. 24, Issue: 3, pp. 269–284.

Bharadwaj S M (1973), *Hindu Places of Pilgrimage in India – A Study in Cultural Geography*, London, University of California Press.

Bhattacharyya N N, (1988), *Ancient Indian History and Civilisation: Trends and Perspectives,* New Delhi : Manohar, pp. 292-98.

Block Duncan (1958), *The Theory of Committee and Election*, Cambridge, Cambridge University Press.

Box G E P., G M. Jenkins and G C Reinsel (1994), *Time Series Analysis. Forecasting and Control*, third edition, Prentice Hall, Upper Saddle River, New Jersey.

Cameron A C and P K Trivedi (1998), *Regression Analysis of Count Data,* Cambridge, New York, Cambridge University Press.

Cameron, A.C. and P.K. Trivedi (1999), "Essentials of Count Data Regression", *Regression Analysis of Count Data,* Cambridge, New York, Cambridge University Press.

Chakraborty D. (2000), *Provincialising Europe: Thought and Historical Difference*, Princeton University Press, Chicago.

Chattapadhyay, Amiyakumar (2005), *Itihasayer Prakkhapota "Baba Taraknath"* (in Bengali), Calcutta, Sree Tara Press.

Chatterjee, Satischandra (1950), *Fundamentals of Hinduism*, Calcutta (Das Gupta).

Chattopadhyay Bhaskar (1998), *Culture of Bengal through the Ages, Some Aspects*, Burdwan, The University of Burdwan.

Damle Y B (1982), *Caste, Religion and Politics in India*, Oxford and IBH Publishing.

David B. Audretsch, Werner Boente and Jagannadha Pawan Tamvada (2007), "Religion and Entrepreneurship", *Jena Economic Research Papers* No. 2007-075, Friedrich-Schiller-University and the Max Planck Institute of Economics, Jena, Germany.

Dehejia. R and Dehejia V H, (1993), "Religion and Economic Activity in India: An Historical Perspective", *American Journal of Economics and Sociology*, Vol. 52, No. 2 (April 1993), pp. 145-153.

Desender K A, Castro C E and Escamilla De León S A, (2011), "Earnings Management and Cultural Values", *American Journal of Economics and Sociology*, Vol. 70, Issue 3 (July 2011), pp. 639-670.

Ghosh, Benoy (1962), *Samuyik Patre Benglar Samaj Chitra* (in Bengali), 1, Calcutta, Bengal Publishers Pvt. Ltd., Kolkata.

Greene, H. William (2003), *Econometric Analysis*, fifth edition, Chapter 21: Models For Discrete Choice and Chapter 22:

Limited Dependent Variable and Duration Models, Prentice-Hall, New York, pp. 663-774.

Gujarati N Damodar (2005), *Basic Econometrics*, McGRAW-HILL International Edition, New Delhi.

Gun M A, Gupta K M and Dasgupta B (2002), *Fundamentals of Statistics* (Vol.1), The World Press Private Limited, Kolkata.

Gupta S P (1993), *Statistical Methods*, New Delhi, Sultan Chand & Sons.

Gupta S C and Kapoor V K (2007), *Fundamentals of Mathematical Statistics*, 11th Edn., (Reprint), Sultan Chand and Sons.

Heilbronen, Robert (1980), *Worldly Philosophers: The Lives, Times and Ideas of the great Economic Thinkers* (5th ed.), New York : Simon and Schuster.

Hiram C Barksdale, Jimmy E Hilliard and Hugh J Guffey Jr. (1974), "Spectral Analysis of Advertising-Sales Interaction", *Journal of Advertising*, Vol. 3, No. 4 (Autumn, 1974), pp. 26-33+39.

Hunter, W W (1876), *A Statistical Account of Bengal*, Vol. 3, Districts of Midnapur and Hugli (including Howrah), London, Trauber & Co.

Husain S Abid (2007), "The Bases of Indian Culture", *The National Culture of India*, National Book Trust, India.

James, R. N. and Sharpe D L (2007), The "Sect Effect" in Charitable Giving: Distinctive Realities of Exclusively Religious Charitable Givers, *American Journal of Economics and Sociology*, Vol 66, iv, pp. 697–726.

Jenkins G M, and D G Watts (1968), *Spectral Analysis and Its Applications*, San Francisco: Holden-Day, *Inc*.

Kaushal, G. (2001), *Economic History of India, 1757 to 1966*, Kalyani Publishars, New Delhi.

Maddala G S (1992), *Introduction to Econometrics*, Second Edition, Macmillan Publishing Company, New York.

Mitra, S K (1968), *Hooghly Jalar Itihas O Benglar Samaj* (in Bengali), 3, Calcutta, Mitrani Prakashani, Kolkata.

Mitra, Sudhirkumar (2007), *Tarakeswar Itikatha* (in Bengali), Calcutta, Calcutta Cultural Centre.

Munger M. (2006), "Preference modification vs. incentive manipulation as tools of terrorist recruitment: The role of culture", *Public Choice*, Vol. 128, No. 1/2, The Political Economy of Terrorism (Jul., 2006), pp.131-146.

Nehru Jawaharlal (2004), *Letters from a Father to his Daughter*, Penguin Book Trust, New Delhi.

Robert H Nelson (2001), *Economics As Religion: From Samuelson to Chicago*, Pennsylvania State University Press (June 2001).

Olfa, Frini and El Lahga, Abdel-Rahmen (2002), "A Socioeconomic Analysis of Fertility Determinants With a Count Data Models: The Case of Tunisia", Conference Paper, Number: 092002023 Cairo, Egypt: *Economic Research Forum for the Arab Countries*, Iran and Turkey (ERF).

Osgood W. (2000), "Poisson-based Regression Analysis of Aggregate Crime Rates.", *Journal of Quantitative Criminology*, 16, pp. 21-43.

Paternoster R. and R. Brame (1997), "Multiple Routes to Delinquency? A Test of Developmental and General Theories of Crime", *Criminology,* 35, pp. 45-84.

Preus, J. Samuel (1987), *Explaining Religion: Criticism and Theory from Bodin to Freud*, New Haven: Yale University Press.

Pritchard, E E Evans (1965), *Theories of Primitive Religion*, Oxford: At the Clarendon Press and New York: Oxford University Press.

Project Report of IDSMT Tarakeswar (2002), Tarakeswar Municipality, West Bengal.

Redfield, Robert (1967), *The Little Community and the Peasant Society and Culture*, Chicago, the University of Chicago Press.

Sen A K (1973), "Behaviour and the Concept of Preference", *Economica,* 40: 241-59.

Sen Amartya (2001), "Many Faces of Gender Inequality" (Article), *Frontline*, Vol. 18, November 9, 2001.

Sen Sukumal (2004), *Bharater Sabhyata O Samajbikashe Dharma Shreni O Jatibhed*, National Book Agency Pvt. Ltd., Kolkata.

Shami Dayananda Saraswati (1975), *Light of Truth*, Sarvadeshik Arya Pratinidhi Sabha, Arya Samaj Foundation Centenary, New Delhi.

Simon Milne and Irena Ateljevic (2001), "Tourism, economic development and the global–local nexus: theory embracing complexity", *Tourism Geographies*, Taylor & Francis Ltd, http://www.tandf.co.uk/journals

Tone Bleie, (2003), "Pilgrim Tourism in the Central Himalayas: The Case of Manakamana Temple in Gorkha", *Nepal Mountain Research and Development*, Vol. 23 No. 2, pp. 177–184.

Photo Gallery

1. Preparation of *'Jal Ghat'*.

2. Congregation of Pilgrims for Darshan of the Deity.

3. Sample of Handicrafts.

4. A View of Dudh Pukur.

5. Municipal Bus Terminus.

6. Tarakeswar Railway Station.

7. Parking Area of Rajbari Ground.

8. Queue of Buses and Truckers at Bus Stand.

9. Congregation of Pilgrims.

10. People Worshipping the Image of Sacred Bull.

Index

A

A Simple Simulation Study, 147
actual visit, 179
administrative activities, 98
administrative inefficiency, 180
agricultural works, 84
amenities, 36
anthropologists, 63
atheists, 60
auspicious months, 48
auspicious seasons, 96
average experience, 122
average experience index, 130
average level of income, 131

B

barriers, 66
behave rationally, 73
Behavioural Variables, 142
beneficiary, 16
beneficiary associates, 99
beneficiary groups, 16, 32, 156
beneficiary groups of cultural agents, 24
benefits, 9
bi-variate data, 85
biasness, 129
boarding and lodging, 89
budget constraint, 135
business organisation, 65

C

capital, 66
Care Economics, 16
care industry, 17
caste composition, 81
caste system, 64
caste-system, 21
casual, 38
categorical variables, 142
Chaitra Sankranti, 29
Chayanov Thesis, 131
choice, 155
Choice Modelling, 69
church attendance, 67
class frequencies, 110
cluster analysis, 69
commercial activities, 41
computer-based iterative variable-selection proced, 142
condensed economic cluster, 151
conditional distribution, 138
conditional mean function, 136
consistent estimates, 138, 139
constraints, 56
consumer participation, 18
consumers (pilgrims), 74
consumers' freedom, 56

consumers of the sacred, 62
consumption, 89
consumption activity, 16
Consumption propensity, 162
contingent behaviour, 68
Contingent Valuation, 69
contingent valuation, 136
continuous distribution, 110
continuous frequency distribution, 110
contractual, 77
contractual tie-up, 40
Cost Variables, 142
costs, 9
count data, 136
Count Data Model, 136
Count Regression Analysis, 134, 144
count regression model, 52
count regression models, 146
covariates, 144
cross-sectional data, 140, 159
cultural economics, 177
cultural experience, 68
cultural factors, 65
cultural feature, 82
Cultural goods, 133
cultural linkage, 69
cultural loss, 69
Cultural Markets, 1
cultural milieu, 133
cultural pace, 156
cultural site, 141
Cultural Space, 157
cultural studies, 141
cultural value, 69
Cultural Worldwide Scale, 69
culture, 16

D

Darshan, 27
Degree of Devotion, 118
degree of devotion, 75, 83, 129
degree of inequality, 173
deity, 23
deity's favour, 78
demand and supply side, 73
demand side, 15
demand-supply interaction, 17
demand-supply mechanism, 133
demographic, 62
demographic factors, 66
Demographic Features, 31
demographic particularities, 111, 159
demography, 19
dependability diligence, 64
dependent variable, 136
Descriptive Statistical Values, 134
descriptive statistics, 163
deviant faiths, 57
devotees, 65, 90
devotion expenditure, 129
Dharna, 30
divine grace, 77

E

earning potential, 164
econometric results, 134
economic behaviour, 15, 156
economic benefits, 101
Economic Culture, 18
economic dependency, 52
economic development, 73, 179
economic growth, 67
economic injustice, 60
economic interdependence, 64
economic motives, 78
economic network, 51
economic progress, 62
economic stability, 76

economic theologian, 62
economic theologians, 62
economic valuation, 69
Economics of Religion, 26
economics of religion, 55
education entertainment, 51
educational qualification, 104
educational status, 116, 169
efficiency to visit, 119, 129
employment, 26
endogeinity, 163
enhance economic performance, 67
entrepreneur, 68
entrepreneurial, 68
environmental effects, 67
ethical foundation, 62
ethical standards, 17
European civilisation, 74
expenditure of, 118
Expenditure Variable, 162
expenses, 36
Experience Index, 90, 91, 103, 105
experience index, 95, 130
experience level, 122, 126, 163
experience pattern, 122
explanatory variables, 142
exponential distribution, 138
Exponential model, 146
Exponential Regression Model, 138
external effect, 17
External effects, 24
external forces, 17
extra income, 99

F

F-tests, 143
factory workers, 84
Family Dependency Ratio, 108
family dependency ratio, 93, 94, 130
family education, 82
festive seasons, 44
field investigation, 71, 111, 128
flexible, 66
frequency curve, 121
frequency of visits, 146
frequency polygon, 110
fulfillment of promises, 64
fundamental assumptions, 57

G

Gajan, 30
Gini co-efficient, 173
Gini co-efficient to examine, 179
God, 59
Government Transport, 49

H

Handicraft, 32
hard-pressed ritual associates, 66
hazard risks, 135
hereditary groups, 90
high-caste people, 21
Hindu pilgrimage, 134
histogram, 110
historic role, 73
historical evidence, 74
homogeneous soio-cultural patterns, 161
homoscedastic variance function, 136
honesty and openness to strangers, 67
hospitalities, 36
hospitality providers, 166
human capital, 165
Human Culture, 18
human decisions, 73

I

Income distribution, 175
Income flow, 9
Income manifold, 100
Income Variables, 161
indispensable factor, 50
individual psyche, 150
individual traits, 67
indoctrination, 56
inequality, 163
inflow, 111
informal services, 77
infrastructural arrangements, 100
infrastructural facilities, 180
infrastructural problems, 180
infrastructure, 68
institutional economics, 55
interview method, 79
intra-temple economic political environment, 24
irrationality, 56
iterative variable-
selection procedures, 162

J

Jal, 30

L

latent variables, 69
law, 50
law and administration, 50
legal conventions, 68
level of satisfaction, 140, 160
literacy levels, 92
literacy rate, 165
literacy structure, 86
literate, 82
literature, 52
livelihood, 9
livelihood opportunities, 156
Local Hospitality Providers, 37
local hospitality providers, 32, 99
log likelihood, 146
Lorenze Curve, 173
low-caste people, 21
lump-sum, 30

M

mainstream economics, 155
manual works, 31
marginal contribution, 148
marginal cost of risk, 135
marginal curves, 148
Marginal Economic Cost, 135
marginal effect, 148, 178
market department, 98
market efficient, 17
market forces constrain, 60
market mechanism, 17
markets, 56
material and spiritual, 59
material problems, 78
material realities, 60
materialistic gains, 78
materialistic wellBeing, 157
mathematical curve, 110
mean-variance equality, 137
menial workers, 34, 84
menial works, 84
mental, 16, 156
micro-level, 69
micro-level analysis, 51, 75
middle-caste groups, 21
modern civilisation, 74
modernisation, 68
monotonous daily life, 78
moral enforcement mechanism, 60
moral prosperity, 73

moral restrictions, 17
morality, 17
multi-collinearity, 142, 162
Multiple Regressions Analysis, 179
Multiplier, 24
Municipal Authority, 47
mythological stories, 25, 33
myths, 25

N

nature, 77
Negative Binomial Count Model, 146
negative binomial distribution, 137
Negative Binomial Maximum Likelihood (ML) specific, 136
Negative Externality, 25
negative externality, 17
negative relation, 67
non-Bengali group, 43
non-economic factor, 59
non-economic factor, religious culture, 110
non-government services, 84
non-quantifiable, 67
non-religious agents, 23
non-ritual articles, 101
non-ritual functions, 88
non-ritual hospitality providers, 147
non-ritual services, 99
non-secular services, 9, 15, 155
Non-temple Culture, 22
non-traditional economic discussion, 71
non-traditional field, 75
Normal Count Model, 139
normal frequency curve, positively and negatively, 111

O

observations, 110
occupational groups, 75
occupational structure, 83, 156
occupational structure, standard of living, 16, 28
occupational structures, 84
one's value, 61
open-ended questionnaire, 79
opiate-based drugs, 61
opium of masses, 60
ordinary economics, 133
Ordinary Least Square Regression, 136, 178
outflow of pilgrims, 111
over-dispersion, 138

P

panel data, 68
parameters, 138
parametric model, 137
parking charge, 37
peak and lean periods, 141
pecuniary gains, 25
Per Capita consumption, 162
per capita cost, 146
per capita family consumption, 166
per capita family income, 166
per capita income, 62, 111
per capita level of income, 93
per capita monthly income, 83
percentage attendance, 81
performance of volition, 83
Permanent, 101
permanent and seasonal traders, 158
permanent employee, 39

Permanent Employees, 98
Permanent employees, 89
Permanent Income, 36
permanent stalls, 42
permanent temple employees, 34
personal interaction, 177
personal materialistic gains, 180
phenomenal height, 76
phenomenon of over-dispersion, 144
philanthropic, 33
philanthropic purposes, 89
physical capital, 165
physical ordeal ceremony, 66
pilgrim, 16
pilgrim component, 76
Pilgrim Guides, 37
Pilgrim guides, 90
pilgrim seasons, 67
Pilgrimage, 80
pilgrimage activity, 76
pilgrimage place, 22
pilgrimage site, 16
pilgrims, 49
pilgrims' behaviour, 111
pilgrims' occupational pattern, 84
pilgrim's utility function, 134
pilgrim's valuation, 135, 147
pilgrims-oriented articles, 101
pleasure of mind, 23
Poisson, 136
Poisson Count Model, 136
Poisson, Exponential count, Normal count, 136
Poisson model, 146
Poisson regression model, 138
Political Culture, 18
popularity, 80
Positional Variables, 142, 161
Positive Externality, 25
positively stimulate economic growth, 66
poverty line, 105
powerhouse, 52
predicted value, 136
predictive covariates, 170
preservation of tradition, 69
priest-craft profession, 94
Priestcraft, 90
priests, 77
primary data, 51, 72, 128
primitive, 65
primitive belief, 69
Private Priests, 37
Private priests, 90
processions, 29
profane object, 27
property concerned disputes, 78
proxy to income, 164

Q

qualities of visit, 134
quantifiable, 67
Quasi-Maximum Likelihood (QML) estimators, 136
Quasi-Maximum Likelihood (QML) Method, 138

R

Railway Authority, 49
random, 111
rational choice, 74
rationality, 56, 65
recreational motives, 78
recreational purposes, 78
redemption of sin, 25
redistribution of resources, 65
regression analysis, 65
regular, 49
regular, casual and seasonal

pilgrim guides, 97
regular pilgrims, 85
relative poverty level, 169
religious, 166
Religious activities, 73
religious activity, 73
religious affinity, 150
religious agents, 98, 157
religious and non-religious services, 75, 111
religious attractiveness, 66, 172
religious beliefs, 64, 67
religious category, 21
religious commodities, 9, 155
religious component, 52
Religious Culture, 19
religious economics, 67
religious endowment, 75
religious endowments, 65
religious establishment, 74, 101
religious establishment and economic appearance of, 51
religious ethnicity, 179
'religious factor', 59
religious faiths, 74, 76
religious festivals, 76
religious firms, 9
religious goods, 74
religious journey, 82
religious kinship, 179
religious liberty, 57
religious markets, 74
religious merit, 25
religious needs, 99
religious occasions, 98
religious particularities, 74
religious pluralism, 63
religious polarisation, 63
religious purposes, 51
religious requirements, 16, 75, 111
religious satisfaction, 111
religious valuation, 134
rent, 37
reticulated sling, 47
revenues, 97
rigorous quantitative documentation, 69
risk premium, 135
ritual and non-ritual associates, 131
ritual and non-ritual functionaries, 158
ritual ceremonies, 89
ritual customs, 76
ritual duties, 78
ritual hospitality providers, 146
ritual roles, 157
road transports, 49
rural people, 114, 129

S

Sacred, 157
sacred and secular (non-sacred) local hospitality, 75
sacred and secular local hospitality providers, 72
sacred associates, 16
sacred centres, 155
sacred ceremonies, 39
Sacred Group, 32, 88
Sacred group, 99
sacred group, 98
sacred specialists, 22
Sada, 30
salvation, 25
sample survey, 134
Satisfaction Variables, 142, 161
satisfactory earnings, 119
satisfactory income, 102

scarcity, rapid socio-economic changes and urbanis, 66
scared valuation, 146
scientific spirit, 65
Seasonal, 101
seasonal employees, 98
Seasonal Income, 36
seasonal pilgrim guides, 39
secondary data, 51
secondary findings, 141
Secular, 157
secular, 9, 65, 155
secular amenities, 99
secular associates, 16
Secular Group, 34, 88
Secular group, 99
secular group, 98
secularisation, 64, 66
secularisation hypothesis, 64
'secularisation' theory, 56
self-employed, 84
Semi-permanent Employees, 34
semi-skilled, 9, 155, 156
simulation study, 52
Sivaratri, 29
social and economic consequences, 73
social and economical association, 75
social background, 76, 82
social, cultural and economic characteristics, 78
Social Culture, 18, 20
social, economic and cultural behaviour of pilgrim, 76
Social, Economic and Positional Variables, 134
social hierarchies, 75
social progress, 73
Social-economic Culture, 71
social-economic infra structural conditions, 156
social-economic infrastructural conditions, 16
socio-cultural behaviour, 82
socio-cultural feature, 82
socio-cultural motives, 78
socio-economic, 66
socio-economic and cultural scenario, 83
socio-economic characteristics, 166
socio-economic conditions, 110
socio-economic dependency, 75
socio-economic development, 74, 177
socio-economic interaction, 140
socio-economic pattern, 16
socio-economic profile, 109
socio-economic upliftment, 74
Socio-economic Variables, 142, 161
socio-scientific study, 56
sociologists, 65
specific class intervals, 111
spectrum, 9
spiritual and material needs, 78
spiritual guidance, 89
spiritual knowledge, 89
spiritual motives, material motives, 78
spiritual satisfaction, 27
spiritual urge, 151
spurring individual behaviour, 67
Sravani, 30
Sravani Purnima, 29
Sravani yatris, 77
standard of living, 156
statistical data of Eastern Railway, 49
statistical investigation, 71

statistical techniques, 52
statistically insignificant, 171
statistically significant, 146, 166
statistics, 65
Stepwise Regression, 142, 163
stochastic dominance, 147, 148
structured and open-ended questionnaire schedules, 111
sub-culture, 22
subsistence, 40, 98
subsistence level of income, 22
subsistence level of living, 102
supply side, 15
supply-and-demand curves, 64
supra-regional employees, 35
sympathisers, 29
sympathy, 17

T

Tarakeswar, 26
taste for freedom, 63
tax, 37
taxes, 26
technological advances, 73
temple, 65
Temple Authority, 32
Temple Culture, 19, 20, 71
Temple Employees, 32
temple employees, 75
temple of 'Taraknath', 27
temple patronage, 134
temple-state relationships, 57
temple's irrigation program, 65
Temporary Employees, 98
Temporary employees, 89
temporary employees, 157
temporary stalls, 42
The Wealth of Nations, 60
theists, 60
therapeutic purposes, 25
tirtha, 27
Tobit Regression, 165
Tobit Regression Analysis, 169, 179
Tobit regression, Multiple regression, 52
Tourists, 32
traders, 101
traditional clientele, 40
traditional clientele association, 77
traditional economic analysis, 74
Traditional Economics, 18
traditional economics, 16
traditional religious beliefs, 64
transitory, 40, 77
Transport Authority, 47
transport authority, 30
travel cost method, 68, 141
treatment of minority, 57

U

un-skilled workers, 9, 155
uncertainty, 114
Unskilled Workers, 157
unskilled workers, 156
urban inhabitants, 81
urban people, 114
urban unit, 156
utilisation, 65
utility, 133, 155
utility function, 135
utility maximisation, 162
Utility Providers, 1

V

value-receptors, 76
vintage position, 41, 100
virtuous people, 29
virtuous pleasure, 16, 156

visit efficiencies, 119
visit efficiency, 129
visitors, 100

W

welfare activities, 96

Y

Yatris, 30